The Me Project

Kathy Lipp

HARVEST HOUSE PUBLISHERS

EUGENE, OREGON

THE ME PROJECT
Copyright © 2011 by Kathi Lipp
Published by Harvest House Publishers
Eugene, Oregon 97402
www.harvesthousepublishers.com

Library of Congress Cataloging-in-Publication Data
Lipp, Kathi, 1967-
The me project / Kathi Lipp.
p. cm.
ISBN 978-0-7369-2966-0 (pbk.)
1. Christian women—Religious life. 2. Self-realization—Religious aspects—Christianity. I. Title.
BV4527.L565 2010
248.8'43—dc22

2010028946

This book is dedicated to my gang of girls:

*Kim Gonsalves—For loving me, praying for me,
cheering me on, and loving the people I love.*

*Shannon Jordahl—For being the inspiration for this book,
and an inspiration to me.*

*Mary Dickerson—For doing motherhood with me, always
accepting me, and always (and I mean always) making me laugh.*

*Vikki Francis—For tangibly caring for me during the hardest
part of my life, and showing me that living with God direction
is the most exciting way to live.*

*And to Angela Bowen—For being my everyday support, my reality
check, and my constant reminder that God is our strength.*

*I am proud and blessed to call each of you friend. Thank you
for helping me to become, every day, a little more of what God
wants me to be. Thank you also for letting me be a part of the
living-breathing God-miracle that is each of you.*

Contents

Acknowledgments

Kimberly—One of my greatest joys in life is to see you pursuing your goals with tenacity and passion. Incredibly proud to be your mom.

Justen—You are a daily inspiration. Your dedication to writing fuels me. Thanks for being my writing buddy at the coffee shop and helping me stay focused. (BTW—I finished the book, so you owe me a Starbucks.)

Amanda—Love seeing you follow the path God has for you.

Jeremy—Every day you're becoming more of the man you were created to be. No one is more determined than you are.

To the Lipps, the Dobsons, and the Richersons—for loving us deeply and unconditionally.

To the women who loved and cheered me on while I was still figuring out who I wanted to be when I grew up: Bea Scott, Karen Kazlauckas, and Linda Ochsenbein.

To the BIC girls (and one guy); Katie Vorreiter, Cathy Armstrong, Shelley Adina, Kirstin Billerbeck, Chris Janssen, Camy Tang, Dineen Miller, and Justen Hunter. Thanks for keeping me faithful to the Orchard Valley Coffee writing club.

To just some of the women who have mentored me along the way: Debbie McDonald, Dee Wilson, Patti Johnston, Kim Meyer, Sue Thayer, Susie Welling, Judy Squier, Karen Porter, Gerry Wakeland, and Jan Coleman. Thank you for investing in me and so many other women. You will never know the impact you have had.

To the women who are walking alongside me in ministry: Susy Flory, Cheri Gregory, Cindi McMenamin, Carole Wolaver, Marla Taviano, Teresa Drake, and Jane Liddle. I'm truly blessed to be on this journey with you.

My ministry partners who walk alongside me—Rachelle Gardner at WordServe Literary; Rod Morris, LaRae Weikert, and the entire team at Harvest House; and Monica Trevino.

Finally, to Roger. Very few people get to experience the daily love, support, prayer, and just plain fun that I do. Thanks for loving me with words and actions and without conditions. Shut the door, baby.

1

Is This All There Is?

*"The future belongs to those who believe
in the beauty of their dreams."*

ELEANOR ROOSEVELT

Is it possible to have a real life and pursue a dream at the same time?

I remember the precise moment that struggle began for me. I had been asked to speak in front of a group of women at church on—of all topics—frozen food. For over a year, I had been cooking big batches of food and then freezing it for my family's meals. When the women's ministry leader heard about my system, she asked me to give a seminar to the ladies at our church. Being the people-pleaser I am, I told her I would be happy to.

Once I hung up the phone, I instantly regretted saying yes and tried to call her back to tell her, "No, I can't do it—and please do not ever call me again." I considered changing churches, just to be safe. Her phone was busy—for the next hour and a half. I took it as a sign that I needed to be a big girl and not cancel.

I spent the next few weeks planning and praying and, on two occasions, throwing up. I was terrified about speaking in front of these women. This was completely uncharted territory for me. I decided I needed to channel my nervous energy, so I frantically typed up recipes, made sample meals for the ladies to try, and rehearsed my presentation in a mirror several times before the "big night."

That evening, something wild and wonderful came over me as I stepped up to the podium. I was no longer nervous—I was exhilarated.

I loved being with these women, teaching, joking, and sharing infor-mation. Several women came up to me that night and the following Sunday to let me know how much they appreciated what I had to share. Later I found out that many of the women had gone shopping the next day to try some of the system in their homes.

That was the moment I knew what I wanted to be when I grew up.

That was also the exact moment I started to feel guilty. The only things I had felt this passionate about before were my God and my family—and it scared me. I didn't want to do anything that would take away from my eagerness to be the kind of woman I was "supposed to be." But, like a beach ball I kept trying to hide underwater, my desire to speak and write kept resurfacing.

I remember, like a woman addicted to a drug, actually praying that God would take those desires away. I wanted to be fully content with how my life was—working, raising kids, being a part of the Parent Teacher Association, serving at church. In my mind, if I was a good mom, a good wife, that should be enough. It was only after several months of prayer and talking to other women about my secret hope that God showed me this was more than my own desire. This was a calling on my life from Him.

You would have thought that would have made me feel a little less guilty. The truth is, it's a constant battle—the balance of living the day-to-day with purpose and growth while following the passion God has placed in my heart.

Is there a way for a woman to pursue her dream that honors God and, at the same time, to balance all the other roles of her life? When I started to talk to other women about this, many of them shared the same secret shame. It's the feeling that the here and now—work, fam-ily, friends, church—is not, in and of itself, enough.

Is it selfish for you to want more, or could it possibly be that the feeling is from God—that you were created to honor God and serve Him in other ways besides caring for a family and bringing home a paycheck?

You may be one of those women who have always known precisely what your passion is. Perhaps, like me, you had your "Oh, that's it!" moment long after being a grown up. Either way, there is a little thrill that bubbles up inside when you think, "Wow, I could do this."

And that is when you start to dream a little. Maybe, just maybe, you can spend some time discovering what God's plan is for your life…that maybe your plan starts with tiny baby-steps today instead of twenty years from now when all the kids are grown and gone or you have climbed the corporate ladder. Maybe that passion that has been simmering and stirring in your soul is something you can work toward, think about, and plan for *right now*.

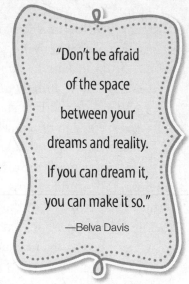

"Don't be afraid of the space between your dreams and reality. If you can dream it, you can make it so."
—Belva Davis

Sounds pretty exciting, doesn't it?

There are days when it all feels possible. On Monday the kids are agreeable (or at least your son is not threatening to sell his little sister's Barbie on eBay to fund his Xbox addiction). The house is reasonably clean. You have matching socks just sitting there in the sock drawer ready to be worn. You even carve out time for some Bible study in the morning. You make it to work four minutes early! You get home and remember that you put something in the Crock-Pot as you left this morning and dinner is waiting. That gives you a moment to peruse the college catalogs, looking at classes that sound absolutely fascinating. You start to think, *I could do this. I could raise wonderful kids, do great work, and have a life too!*

And then on Tuesday another reality sets in.

On Tuesday the dog chews the head off your daughter's Barbie and through the cords of your son's Xbox. Since the kids have *nothing to do* because of the Barbie/Xbox massacre, they decide to finally team up, leaving your house in the wake of their destructive path. After looking at the pile of unwashed clothes on your left and the empty dresser drawers on your right, you think, *Matching socks are so last year*, and go for a holiday theme of one Rudolph and one Santa sock—at least both their noses light up. Your Bible just sits there, reminding you it gets opened up a lot less than your secret container of rocky road ice cream stashed behind the frozen vegetables in the back of the freezer. Your boss cannot figure out why you are always so stressed out when you come in for work. Dinner is a drive through the Golden Arches—again. When you finally get the mail, you see the new college course catalogs staring you in the face, openly mocking you: "Just 14 more years until your kids are off to college, and then you can start taking classes right along with them."

I understand the Tuesday reality. I have lived the above paragraph. I have also come to the conclusion there is hope.

Friend, God has a plan only you can live out—you are specifically designed for it. And that plan is designed to bring you closer to God, to honor Him, and to bring you joy. As the apostle Paul said, "It's in Christ that we find out who we are and what we are living for. Long before we first heard of Christ…he had his eye on us, had designs on us for glorious living, part of the overall purpose he is working out in everything and everyone" (Ephesians 1:11 MSG).

The purpose of *The Me Project* is to help you accomplish just that—to help you determine not only what your God-given talents and passions are, but also to come up with realistic steps and a timeline to help you achieve all God intends for your life. To quote one of our favorite branches of the military, the purpose of this book is to help you *be all that you can be*.

Listen, this isn't about being everything to everybody. There are dozens of books on the market that say, "You can have it all! You can do it all!" You and I both know what the problem with that is—it just doesn't work. But there's a big difference between devoting yourself to being a great mother, wife, and worker and giving up on your dreams completely.

I want to share with you some of the ideas, strategies, and most of all changes in perspective I as well as other women have gone through to live a life designed by God. We can serve Him and our families, friends, and employers with joy. You will meet women who have pursued their dream while raising kids and others who have waited until later in their life. Some have held full-time jobs and pursued their passion in the stolen moments around their careers. One thing they all have in common—a desire to seek after God's heart and to find a plan He has designed uniquely for them.

8) Get a massage.

2

Why *The Me Project?*

Have you ever heard an author say if she could write only one book in her life that book would be...It's the book the author believes she was put here on earth to write. It's the book she dreamed of as she sat behind her computer writing press releases for nonprofit companies or answering phones or going to school or any of the other myriad activities writers do until they get to work on that dream project—that one book.

What you hold in your hands is my one book.

This is the book I have been writing through a marriage, then being a single mom, and now as a wife in a blended family. I've worked as a sales rep, a school secretary, a director of development, and now, finally, as a speaker and writer. Before getting to write this, my one book, I wrote two other books (which I loved), have spoken at hundreds of events, and have written dozens of articles.

My life has not taken the path that I had expected, hoped for, or dreamed about, but it is exactly what I needed to go through, cry through, and experience in order to write what I wanted to write about pursuing the life God wants all of us to live.

And pursuing that kind of life is what I want for you. *The Me Project* is a 21-day guide for dreaming dreams about your life and then setting some goals to make one of those dreams a reality.

Becoming an Expert on Your Life

Several years ago, my husband attended a church leadership conference where a nationally known pastor and his staff were teaching. The attendees were almost all pastors and lay leaders from across the country who had sacrificed time and money, work hours and time away from family in order to attend.

This church had seen an explosion of growth and influence over the previous year—and nobody knew that better than the people who were teaching. At one point, the lead pastor said something along the lines of: "I am successful and you are not. If you want to be successful, you will listen to me and do what I am telling you to do." Let me just say, Roger has not been back to that conference.

"What life has God uniquely created *me* for?"

I never want to buy (or waste time reading) another book with the theme: "I have done this perfectly. If you want to do it perfectly too, do what I say." Rarely, if ever, does life work out in a neat three-point outline for the people I know who are living out the plans God has for them.

Life is messy. There is no straight line between you and what God wants you to do. But the people I've interviewed who have listened to God's leading, followed His path, and are living the lives He has shaped for them share a lot in common. You'll see a lot of those common traits surface in this book.

The Me Project

The Me Project was born out of my need to explore everything God had in store for me—not just as a wife and mom, employee and volunteer. I needed to spend some hard, concentrated time trying to answer the question, "What life has God uniquely created *me* for?"

We never have one role in life. We are never just a mom or just a wife, just an employee or just a volunteer. There are the dozens (if not hundreds) of other things we do that make up who we are. Each of those little roles, if part of God's plan, is valuable and important, deserving of time and energy and attention. The mosaic of roles makes us who we were created to be.

Plus, it's just fun. Let's say the area you want to explore is real estate, but right now your job has you as a marketing assistant at an engineering firm. You might think it would be too much to work and go to classes at the same time. But anytime I have ever explored something I'm passionate about, it gives me energy. Passion is a powerful thing, and you may have reserves that you don't even realize.

The Me Project is by far my most personal book. Every time a woman has come up to me and said, "I want to be a writer (or speaker). Can I take you out to coffee so we can talk about it," I've wished I had this book to give to her (while graciously accepting the latte at Starbucks).

As you read this book, my prayer for you is that in these pages and in these projects, you will have the unusual opportunity to think and pray about what God has designed especially for you. That you will not worry for the moment about how to be a better mom or a better wife (I have other books for those projects...) or even how to be a better Bible study girl. I want you to be a little more self-focused than that. I want you to spend some concentrated time figuring out every little bit of life that God has for you and what He wants you to do about it.

Since none of our paths are going to look the same, it's hard to give specific advice. But on these pages you will see what I have done to create the life I am living right now. It has taken me a long time to believe that, "Yes, in many ways I am on the road to where God wants me to be. And the places I'm not? Well, at least now I'm asking the questions about the next step."

God already knows the plans He has for you. Jeremiah 29:11 says, "For I know the plans I have for you," declares the LORD, "plans to prosper you and not to harm you, plans to give you hope and a future." One of our big jobs here on earth is to figure out what those plans are.

3

But I Don't Have Any Goals
(Or I Have Too Many and Don't Know Where to Start)

Before diving into this book, I want you to spend a little time dreaming and scheming. I want you to figure out a whole bunch of goals for you and your life, pick one, and get started on it. And I want you to start a 50/50 Journal.

Let me tell you a little about my 50/50 Journal. I'm not really sure what prompted me to start it. At the time, I was at a crossroads—newly married, combining our little family with my husband's family, moving to a new city, quitting my job. I felt like I was on the brink of… what, I wasn't quite sure.

I'm a serial journaler. In my years walking on this planet, I have left an impressive number of journals in my wake. I'm great at starting a journal; not so great about the follow-through.

But I'm a sucker for a cute journal. There's something so romantic about a private place to keep my thoughts and dreams. Each time I'm in a bookstore, I can't help but peruse the journal section, dreaming about the beautiful things I would write on the thick paper of that gorgeous, leather-bound book. Or maybe the bright orange and green floral journal with the matching pen. Oh, the possibilities.

That's how it went on the day I met my new journal. With its dark red cover and Irish proverb on the front, it not only matched my mood, it matched my hair color and heritage at the same time. It was love at first sight.

After purchasing the journal and a hazelnut latte, I curled up in one of the bookstore chairs to…what I didn't know.

I didn't want this to be just another journal to be tucked under my bed after I lost interest. I wanted this journal to be different. I spent almost half an hour staring at a blank page.

I dreamt about what I wanted my life to look like. If I knew I was going to live another 50 years, what would I want those 50 years to look like? What would I like to say I had done with that time?

So, I just started to write everything down. I figured that if I was healthy and stayed out of the way of people talking on cell phones while driving, it was conceivable that I *could* have another 50 years on this planet. I started to write down 50 things I wanted to accomplish in the next 50 years. (Actually, I got to 48 things I wanted to accomplish, but made myself think of 2 more since a 50/50 Journal sounds so much cooler than a 50/48 Journal.)

Somehow this new journal was different than the ones I had started before. This was not a daily recitation of deep thoughts that I had while walking on the beach (which is how I imagined everyone else filled their journals). This felt big, important, and all for me.

I wrote down all the things I had dreamed about doing…someday. Some of the items that I included would not be a surprise to anyone:

- To have a deep and growing relationship with God

- To have a close, loving, and God-honoring relationship with my husband

- To have a close, loving, and God-honoring relationship with my kids

But there was also an impressively long list of goals I had never dared to say out loud. Just a few of the things I put on my list:

- Be on TV

- Take a gourmet cooking class

- Get my nails done once a week

- Travel around the United States for a month without a schedule

I felt silly writing some of those goals down. Getting my nails done once a week seemed less like a goal and more like self-indulgence. "Take a gourmet cooking class" sounded a little frivolous as well. But I had promised myself that I was going to be very free in what I wrote down; I would not censor myself because a goal seemed silly or trivial. I trusted that these goals were between me and God, and I asked Him to bless me in the goals that were within His will and to take away the desire for the ones that may not be from Him.

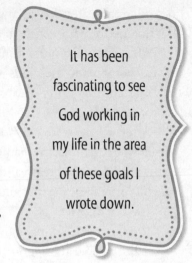

It has been fascinating to see God working in my life in the area of these goals I wrote down.

It has been fascinating to see God working in my life in the area of these goals I wrote down. About once a month, I peruse the list and update any progress I've made toward each goal. It can be as simple as buying a book on cross-country travel. I make a note of it on the page that has "Travel around the United States for a month without a schedule" as the goal. Any progress is noted and celebrated.

Not long after starting my list, I met one of my most daring goals. I was invited to speak in a little church about an hour from home. Traffic was light, so I had time to stop at a Starbucks and grab a latte before heading over to the meeting. I took a few minutes in the parking lot to pray for the event I was about to speak at. "God," I prayed, "I don't know these women or this church, but I pray there would be fruit from this meeting. I commit our time and these ladies into Your hands."

When I arrived at the church, I did a double take to make sure I was at the right spot. The name on the building matched the name in my appointment book—but my car was the only one in the parking lot. After trying to call the meeting planner to figure out where I was supposed to be, a lone car finally joined me in front of the church.

I called out to the driver, "Is this where the moms' event is being held?"

She assured me it was and that everyone just must be running late.

I carried my props and handouts into the auditorium that was obviously set up for hundreds. In the nearby kitchen a team of people was cooking meals for the elderly, and a couple of maintenance men were setting up for whoever the next group was.

After about 25 more minutes, two more ladies showed up. These three women and their kids were my whole audience.

The country song "I Shaved My Legs for This?" kept running through my brain.

After a brief introduction (where the woman introducing me couldn't remember my name and didn't know what I was speaking on), I took a deep breath and gave my speech as if I were delivering it to 300 instead of the tiny audience sitting in front of me.

It was a disaster.

People were clanking in the kitchen, and one of the little boys in my audience looked at his mom and asked in an exasperated tone, "When is she going to stop talking?"

Trust me buddy, I wanted it to be over just as badly.

When I finished, one of the ladies (the one who still couldn't remember my name) said thanks and showed me to the door. I climbed back into my car, then paused for a moment and started praying.

"Really, God, what was that all about? That is probably the worst speaking engagement I have ever had. I prayed and committed the time to You."

Just as I was finishing my grumpy little prayer, this tiny woman comes running up to my van and knocks on my window. As I stepped out of the car, she blurted, "Hi, my name is Arlene. I was passing through as you were speaking, and I just loved what you had to say. I know this is coming out of left field, but I have a local cable TV show on parenting and was wondering if you might be a guest on it."

I was sure I could hear God laughing.

In my 50/50 Journal, every small step is recorded and celebrated. It is my personal record of how deeply interested God is in delighting me by first putting desires in my heart, and then blessing me by fulfilling those desires.

We all have these nebulous goals in our life that we want to accomplish, someday. If you have never taken the time to commit them to paper, do it today. There is power in writing your goals down. They become concrete and tangible. The goals are easier to break down into smaller steps, giving you a real chance to see those dreams become a reality.

Once you have captured some of your dreams in this journal, I'm going to ask you to pick one of them and turn it into a goal—and that's where we get started with *The Me Project*.

Getting Started with *The Me Project*

Nine Quick Steps (I Promise—They Really Are Easy!)

1. Pick a goal—any goal.

As I said in the previous chapter, I'm going to ask you to spend some time brainstorming about the dreams you have for your life. Then I'm going to ask you to pick one of those dreams and turn it into a goal to work on in this book.

2. Get a journal.

If you are like every other woman I know, you probably have a dozen or more journals lying around your house. Grab one of those, or a college notebook, or go buy yourself a pretty journal you know you will love to look at for years to come.

3. Read through all the projects.

This is your chance to get a feel for all 21 of the projects. Be sure to use all of this book—make notes in the margins, scribble and doodle on the pages, and start to think about ways to tailor each project to your situation.

4. Find two friends (at least) to do the projects with you.

It doesn't matter if they're phone friends, Internet buddies, or face-to-face girlfriends you meet with at Starbucks down the street. Location is not important; consistency is. Figure out a time to spend together (after everyone has read through the book) to come up with a plan for when and how you're going to do the projects.

If you're doing this as a group, be sure to check out all the free group resources on our website www.ProjectsForYourSoul.com. You'll find lots of great tools, forms, and other fun stuff to make this a great group project.

5. Sign the Accountability Covenant (page 35).

6. Decide on a start date.

It can be tomorrow or two weeks from now. Mark it in a big bold way on your kitchen calendar. Set up reminders on your computer. I recommend that you give yourself a couple of days to get ramped up and pull together a plan that you're excited about.

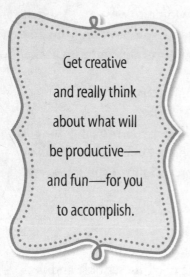

Get creative and really think about what will be productive—and fun—for you to accomplish.

7. Come up with your plan.

You decide what steps you're going to take each day. I've provided a variety of ideas, but it's up to you to decide how you'll carry out each day's project.

Get creative and really think about what will be productive—and fun—for you to accomplish. In the space provided, write down in advance what you're going to do for each day. When I am fixing dinner each night, it's not the cooking that's so hard—it's trying to figure out what to have for dinner (that's why every grocery store is jam packed at 4:30 in the afternoon). First, plan your work and then work your plan.

You will also need to think in advance about managing the project and your real life. Do you want to audit a class at the local community college? Then arrange today for the babysitter instead of the night before. Want to buy a new set of paintbrushes? Then you'll want to cut back on the grocery budget for a couple of weeks to get what you need. (Who said a steady diet of mac-n-cheese was a bad thing?)

8. Share your project plan with your accountability partners.

I recommend that you make copies of your calendar to share with your accountability partners. There is a Project Planner for you to use on page 208. That way, you can commit to pray for each other, as well as lend support on days that may be particularly challenging. Who knows, your partners may have some great, creative ideas to share.

9. Be flexible.

If one of the projects doesn't line up with your life, swap it for another day. If you're going on vacation for a couple of days, then you could postpone *The Me Project* or double up on some days before you go. The intention of *The Me Project* is not to add stress but to lead you to the life you were designed for. Just do something, intentionally, every day.

Starting Your Own 50/50 Journal

Buy a journal that you love and that inspires you. Spend a little money to get one that you wouldn't mind carrying around for the next 50 years. Or if you're on a budget and don't mind something old-school, use your kid's spiral notebook from science class that she never used. Make sure it has at least 120 pages in it and that it's large enough to doodle and dream in.

Buy a great pen to keep with your journal. If you are artistic, you may want to use different colored pens, pencils, or whatever it takes to make your dreams come to life on the page.

Spend some time writing down dreams as they come to you. Number each dream and write it at the top of the page, giving you at least two pages (front and back) for each goal. You will need all that room to write down the steps you're taking to accomplish that dream, as well as all the "God steps" that are happening to make that dream a reality.

Give yourself time. Dreaming may be a new exercise for you. Perhaps you cannot come up with all 50 goals at the same time. That's OK. Allow space in your journal for God to lay new dreams on your heart. If you are a perfectionist, you might feel more free by "brain-dumping" on some scratch paper and then transferring those goals into your notebook.

Update. As often as you are inspired to (but at least once a month) go through your journal and write down all of the steps you've taken toward your various goals. Some may have been very deliberate steps (buying European travel guides for your goal "Travel throughout Europe for a month") while some may be "God steps"—things that line up in ways that can be explained only as God's working (your community center has started a watercolor class the same week that you write "Learn to watercolor" in your journal).

Wait on God instead of going for your goal. Since starting my journal, I have already seen some of my dreams become reality ("Appear on TV," "Learn gourmet cooking"), while some I have not taken one step toward ("Visit Germany for two weeks"). Sometimes we need to wait on God for the right goal at the right time. As I see God working in so many areas of my life, it's easier to wait on Him in the areas I need to.

Picking Your Goal

Now that you've started your 50/50 Journal, I want you to pick one goal, any goal, and use that goal to get started on your Me Project journey. Here are some things I want you to consider:

Pick a goal that's not too hard. I want you to experience some victory in achieving your goals. If one on your list is "Become a doctor," that might be a little intense for your first, out-of-the-gate goal. I'm not saying that can't be a goal, but I would love to see you start with something that isn't going to take 12 years of your life.

But don't pick something that's too easy either. If one of your goals is to make sure you send a birthday gift to your mom, on time, every year—good for you! (As a mom, I heartily endorse this goal.) However, what you need to achieve this goal is a friend who will hold you accountable, not a three-week program.

Dream big. This book is all about getting started on your dreams, not completing them within three weeks. So don't be too safe. Pick something that's going to take more than three weeks to accomplish. Here are some goals for you to consider the first time out. Remember, your purpose is not to complete these goals but to get the ball rolling.

- Learn to decorate cakes
- Learn to lead a Bible study
- Change job industries
- Walk a 5K
- Get your house organized
- Train your dog
- Plant a garden
- Create a retirement plan
- Learn to cook organically
- Write a magazine article
- Start a girl band
- Get a belt in karate
- Get a new job
- Redecorate a room

5

Accountability
The Key to Making It All Work

We have all bought books that we were sure were going to change our life. I have several books that I bought with the best of intentions, but the spines on them have never been cracked. The way to make *The Me Project* work is to make sure you have women in your life who will cheer you on when you are accomplishing your goals and hold your feet to the fire when you want to give up.

That's why I don't want you to go on this journey alone. Just like the best road trips, the best journeys in life are better when you have some friends along.

So before you start on the projects, get a friend or two (or four) to sign up with you. I mean, really, what better gift can you give a friend than to ask her to join you to accomplish one of her dreams?

Take some time to look over the accountability agreements and how you can support each other. Is it daily phone calls as you check off your projects? Once-a-week Skype meetings with your friends to check on each other's progress? Together decide what will be most effective for your group.

Everyone does better at achieving when they know someone is checking in on them. If you want to see your dreams become a reality, make sure you have a couple of good, honest friends to help you get there.

The Me Project Accountability Covenant

The Covenant

We, the readers of *The Me Project,* enthusiastically agree to enter into an encouraging relationship with each other for the sole purpose of engaging in and completing all projects to intentionally work toward a goal. As the encouragement crew, we vow to:

- Encourage each person in our crew.

- Check in with each other at least once a week.

- Put our plans on paper and discuss them with each other.

- Laugh only *with* each other, not *at* each other.

- Pray for each other every day for the 21 days.

- Keep details confidential. What we discuss with our encouragement crew stays with our encouragement crew.

- Ask for help, motivation, or inspiration if we're having a rough time with any part of *The Me Project.*

We the undersigned acknowledge and agree to the terms of *The Me Project* Accountability Covenant on this _____ day of _____, 20____.

_____
Project Manager (You!)

_____
Accountability Partner

_____
Accountability Partner

6

Glossary of Terms

Daily Project

A provided activity by which you'll take a step forward to accomplish this dream that God has planted in your heart. There are 21 *Daily Projects* throughout the book.

Project Manager

You are the only one who is going to make this happen (with God's guidance, of course), so when I refer to the *Project Manager*—that's you, baby.

Accountability Partner

Someone who helps keep your feet to the fire—*The Me Project* fire, that is. *Accountability Partners* join you in this project to collectively discuss your plans and goals, provide enthusiasm, inspiration, and maybe a little laughter along the way.

Project Reports

Some of the earliest *Project Managers* put *The Me Project* to the test and gladly shared some of their success stories. Not only are they entertaining to read, but you can find some inspiring ideas too. *Project Reports* are highlighted at the end of each *Daily Project*.

Getting Creative

Unique, fresh, and specific ideas…just what you need to help you complete each *Daily Project*. Sometimes the hardest part in running the race is getting off the starting block. To help you over this potential hurdle, each *Daily Project* features a *Getting Creative* section to get you motivated and mobilized to get moving!

Getting Down to Business

Launching
The Me Project

The Send-Off

Congratulations! I'm so excited that you have decided to take some time and figure out the places that God wants you to go and who He wants you to be.

I know that there are going to be days when life seems so overwhelming, that trying to read a book and work on a project is going to feel overwhelming. But the reality is that you are the only one who gets to decide who you are going to be when you grow up.

In this journey I have two prayers for you.

My first prayer for you is that each and every day God gives you that extra reserve of strength to push through. What I know for sure is this: God has some amazing discoveries for you to make about the you that you are designed to be.

My second prayer is that as you create the life that God intended for you to live, you will feel His pleasure every step of the way.

Kathi Lipp

Week One Projects

Project 1

What Do You Want from Me?
Knowing God's Will for All the Parts of Your Life

"Your talent is God's gift to you.
What you do with it is your gift back to God."

LEO BUSCAGLIA

Your Project

Spend some time recognizing the ways you have sensed God's direction in pursuing this goal. These will be great to reflect back on when you feel discouraged or overwhelmed.

Be Careful What You Ask Your Friends to Pray For

"I need you to keep praying because I don't like what God's telling you."

OK, probably not the most spiritual response I've ever had. But my friend Vikki was just bugging me, listening to God and all.

You see, after 13 years of marriage, I went through a very painful divorce. I found myself with two preteen kids, a pile of debt, and a cloud of depression that overwhelmed me to the point of not being able to move.

While the divorce came with a mix of pain and relief, other circumstances in my life were painful as well.

When I separated from my husband, I needed to find full-time work to support me and my kids. That meant giving up the writing and speaking I had been pursuing. The divorce broke my heart on so many levels, for me and for my kids. But one area that I felt I couldn't discuss with anyone was the fact that I wasn't going to be able to speak and write.

That I should even be thinking about myself and my hopes and dreams just felt so trivial with everything else going on. It seemed selfish to even care about those things because everything else that I loved was lying shredded and in tatters on the floor.

But it grieved me that, in my mind, God was closing the door on my dream.

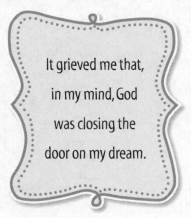

It grieved me that, in my mind, God was closing the door on my dream.

Really, God? I thought. *Everything gets taken away? Why did You even let me think I could be a speaker or a writer? Does everything I care about—my marriage, my family, my dreams—have to be taken away all at once?* I was angry with God and sad and overwhelmed by all the destruction I was facing.

But I didn't have a lot of time to mourn my lost ministry. Mama needed a job—and fast. Notice I didn't say I wanted a job; I needed one. I wasn't interested in a challenging job or one that grew my skills. I was looking for cold, hard cash.

The problem? I wasn't remotely qualified for any occupation that didn't require a hairnet. I had done sales in the past and loved it, but I couldn't wait three months for the commission checks to dribble in. I needed cash. And fast. But besides sales, I really had no other job experience.

The previous couple of years I had been homeschooling my kids and speaking and writing sporadically. I was so sad (OK, downright bitter) that I had to give all that up to get a job. A job that I knew I was probably going to hate.

My kids and I bunked at my mom and dad's house while I started applying for jobs. I was in a strange town, without my friends or church family, without an income. I applied for every job I could think of: receptionist, intake coordinator at the hospital, data input, customer service. I filled out applications, went to interviews, scoured the Internet, and circled jobs in the paper. I was coming up empty and starting to panic.

And then it happened—I got not one job offer but three.

One offer was a sales rep position in the gift industry, but I've already mentioned my problem with working on commission. I needed to look at other options.

The second job was working at a nonprofit legal agency whose primary ministry was defending religious freedoms. While I believed in the cause, my main job would have been data input and client correspondence. While it would provide a paycheck within a couple of weeks, it was not a dream job.

The last job, however, seemed a lot closer to what I would love to do. The gig was selling air time for a Christian radio station. I would get to be in my car, on the move, not tied to a desk. I would get to meet with clients, set my own hours, and it paid a base salary plus commission. Score!

I loved the idea of being a radio girl, and I was so excited about all the people I was going to meet and the fun I was going to have getting to know my new town.

But I also knew that I should probably pray about this new venture, even though my mind was pretty well made up. So I prayed, and I asked some of my closest friends to pray as well.

Big mistake. Big. Huge.

As my friends started to pray, they kept coming back to the job at the legal agency. You know, the boring job. Every time I would gently (or not so gently) steer the conversation back to the radio job, my friends kept saying things like, "Really? Every time I pray for you, God keeps bringing up the legal job."

They were getting pretty annoying.

The problem? I was sensing the same thing. Again, God and I had to have another little chat.

Really, God? But this radio job just seems like it would be a whole lot more fun. And You know what? I could use some fun in my life. Is that too much to ask? It's been a hard couple of years. Couldn't I just have a job I look forward to getting up and going to in the morning?

Yes, when I talk with God it's possible I come off sounding like a spoiled brat.

Since it was so obvious what I needed to do, I did it—I took the job at the legal agency. And then I pouted.

I would love to say that I showed up for work on Monday and it was all lollipops and unicorns. But it was spreadsheets. Lots and lots of spreadsheets.

Shoot. Me. Now.

I hate spreadsheets. But apparently God, in all His wisdom, saw fit to have me do spreadsheets.

After a few weeks of putting little numbers in little boxes, I thought I would go mad. That was until one of my bosses asked me if I would be willing to write an article for the upcoming newsletter. Hey, anything to get away from those little boxes.

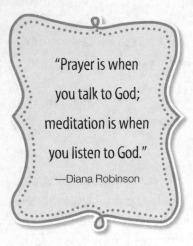

"Prayer is when you talk to God; meditation is when you listen to God."

—Diana Robinson

After a while, I started doing more writing—donor letters, press releases, client letters. Lots of time away from the little boxes.

After a few months, the president of the company was being asked to speak out of state more and more. Eventually, he needed someone to speak at some local and statewide events, and he asked me if I would be willing to.

More time away from the little boxes? I'm in!

After six months, I stopped and thought, *Hey, half my time on this job is spent speaking and writing!*

Yes, I'm a little slow sometimes.

In obeying God, even when I so didn't want to, not only was I able to provide for me and my kids, I also received some direct confirmation that my life as a speaker and author was not over.

Not only did I get to speak and write in that job, I also learned several practical skills that prepared me for this ministry I'm now in—creating newsletters, working with mailing lists, blogging, event planning.

Looking for Confirmation

What does confirmation look like for you? I asked my friend Katie what that confirmation, that leading, looked like for her as she decided to do a year-long mission to a war-torn country in 2004. Here are some of the steps that led her from a safe job as a nurse practitioner in San Jose, California, to traveling a world away doing relief work and church planting in a Muslim country.

1. The seed of a thought is planted.

Katie attended Urbana 2000, a missions conference in Urbana, Illinois. At that conference she heard a missionary speak about evangelizing the Muslim community. Until that point, Katie had always considered Muslim society closed to the gospel.

2. Pay attention.

Katie had always been interested in missions, but didn't know what her next move should be. I love the advice that one of her friends gave her about sensing God's direction: "Pay attention to the things you're noticing because that is often how God speaks."

Katie started to notice more and more that the Muslim world collided with Katie's world. From missionary letters to the evening news, Katie couldn't turn around without noticing her heart growing more tender toward the Muslim people.

3. Holy curiosity is awakened.

Katie said, "It was at that point I developed a holy curiosity." I love that. She knew it was more than a coincidence—she knew that God was steering her in a certain direction and that she better pay attention.

4. Take the first step.

Katie attended a conference in Indiana in 2003 that was focused on evangelizing Muslims.

5. Make the decision.

When Katie received an e-mail from a friend about the opportunity to serve overseas for a year, she was prepared. She had followed God's leading all along the way, and she was ready to take on that adventure with Him.

Your project for today is to write down all the ways that God has confirmed your working on this particular goal. Here are just some of the ways He may have done that:

- Other people you respect have told you to pursue it.

- You feel peace as you give up other activities in order to work on this goal.

- Other people recognize this talent in you and want you to use it.

- You see "divine appointments" show up in your life. You meet a friend of a friend who is looking for an apprentice in the field you are exploring. Just when you need a certain piece of equipment, your friend posts on Facebook that they are getting rid of said piece of equipment.

- As you do your regular Bible study, God keeps whacking you over the head with verses that support what you have been praying about.

I want you to spend just a few minutes writing down all the ways that God has used your past, your present, your friends, your family, your prayers, and His Word to confirm this goal:

And what if you don't believe you've received confirmation? Stop working and start praying.

If you're still wondering if this is a goal you should pursue, and you don't think you're hearing from God, consider a time fast. I love what my friend Mimi Moseley's church instigated in order to be more attuned to God's call on their lives: "Our church challenged us to give up something that took our time and masked our hearing the voice of God. We called it Vox Dei (voice of God). I gave up *Good Morning America* for one month and spent the time I would have watched it in prayer."

Take some time out to pray, and then sit and listen. Eliminate some of the noisemakers in your life that might be masking God's voice.

Prayer for Today

Dear God, I don't want to be one step outside of Your will. Please make me aware of You each step of the way as I pursue what I believe You are calling me to. Let me be sensitive to Your promptings to press on, to wait, and to listen to You.

Getting Creative

- Keep a notepad in your purse or on your cell phone, and when a confirmation comes along, write it down.

- Keep a list of confirmations in your journal. It will be so much fun to go back and see all the places God has intervened on your behalf. These are things you will forget six months from now, so it's important to keep writing them down.

- Consider fasting from a noisemaker in your life. TV? Audio books while walking the dog? Radio while you're in the car? Make sure you are making space to hear God's voice every day.

Project Reports

"When I was first writing and struggling with the reality of what it would take to get published, I took one morning to pray and fast about whether I should keep writing. God led me to Isaiah 58, which is a chapter on fasting. As I read verse 8, I sensed the Holy Spirit telling me to pay keen attention to the end of this verse, and I broke down in tears as I understood God's answer.

'Then your light will break forth like the dawn,
    and your healing will quickly appear;
then your righteousness will go before you,
    and the glory of the LORD will be your rear guard.'

"He's been my rear guard ever since and has blessed my writing greatly."—Dineen

"Just this week, I was praying about what to do with the CIC ministries (a prison ministry I'm involved with). When I met with the chaplain a few hours later, she steered me in a totally different direction than our original one. I will now be the volunteer 'eyeglasses' chaplain, responding to the senior and special placement inmates' requests for reading glasses. I cannot tell you how pleased I am about this, and how it has confirmed that I still need to be involved with this ministry."—Kathy

Your Plan for the Project *(copy your plan on* The Me Project Planner *at the back of this book)*

Results

Project 2

Less Than Perfect
Lessening Your Load

"The thing that is really hard, and really amazing, is giving up on being perfect and beginning the work of becoming yourself."

ANNA QUINDLEN

Your Project

Find another area of your life that you can cut back, do less well, or give up altogether—either permanently or just for the duration of *The Me Project*.

One of the things that I knew I wanted to do as a mom was to feed my kids fresh, healthy food. My kids were born in the early nineties so words like *organic* and *locavore* were not part of this mom's vocabulary. However, when my kids were still in diapers, I made my own baby food and read everything I could about feeding my kids healthy, fresh, and nurturing food.

And then I went back to work.

While my standards hadn't changed, my schedule had. I wanted to keep feeding my family incredibly healthy food. But I would come home after a long day, exhausted from meeting work needs, and realize that this Mother Hubbard's cupboards were bare.

And then suddenly, the Golden Arches seemed like the healthiest option.

When someone suggested that I make meals on the weekend, freeze them, and then pull them out during the week to cook for dinner, initially I balked. I didn't want to feed *my* family frozen food. No. I was going to cook healthy, fresh, nurturing food.

And the vicious cycle of perfectionism, guilt, and ordering food through a loudspeaker continued.

I finally broke down and gave freezer cooking a try. And I am here to testify, honey, it changed my life.

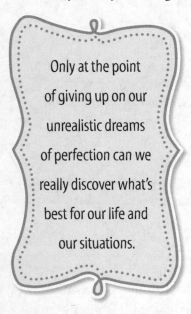

Only at the point of giving up on our unrealistic dreams of perfection can we really discover what's best for our life and our situations.

Here I am, 14 years later, still spending a weekend every other month filling up my freezer with meals that my family really loves. Do I wish that I could shop locally at farmers' markets, bring my bounty home, and create organic meals every night for an appreciative family? Sometimes. But the reality is I have a healthy, nutritious meal on the table most nights. My kids are healthy and even sometimes appreciative. Is it perfect? No. Is it better? Oh yeah.

After giving up on perfection when it came to dinner times, I was able to figure out the best reality for feeding my family. These silly frozen meals have kept me from stressing out. I have even written a booklet on freezer cooking, do seminars for women's groups, and at one point had a meal swap with five other women. (We called ourselves Six Chicks Freeze and Fix.)

Only at the point of giving up on our unrealistic dreams of perfection can we really discover what's best for our life and our situations. I think that most women I know have this in some area of their lives. Say that your area of perfection is a clean house. You have unrealistic ideas of how clean your floors need to be. You spend hours looking through decorating magazines, and you see how perfect everyone else's house is. So you do one of two things:

1. Spend an unreasonable amount of time making sure that everything is perfect. As a result, there will never be time to do any of those activities that really feed your soul.

2. You know that you can never live up to your own idea
of perfection, so you give up before you even start, leaving your house in a shambles. You're frustrated that you
will never have the freedom to do what you want because,
wow, if you can't even keep up on your house, how can
you possibly do _____ .

I spend a lot of time silently comparing myself to my friends and
how they live, and let me tell you, I don't do it because I want to feel
superior to them. I almost always feel like the loser when I line up
myself against anyone else. But I also know that my friends who have
great bodies (because they actually make it to the gym instead of just
paying the $39.99 a month for the privilege of carrying around the
membership card) or super-clean houses or organized filing systems
have their own sets of frustrations and problems. Really, that is what I
tell myself so that I can sleep at night.

(And on a small side note, one of the happiest, most freeing days of
my life was the day my sister-in-law Lucinda and I were chatting about
how in the world other people keep their houses so clean. She told me
she had asked several of her friends who had spotless homes, and every
one of them admitted to having someone come in to clean for them.
I can't tell you what a relief that was to know that I wasn't a slob; I just
didn't hire the right help.)

It's so important to have a realistic picture of your life. If you haven't
been exercising and suddenly decide you're going to work out at the
gym for 90 minutes every day, we all know that isn't going to work.
Even saying you're going three times a week for an hour each day is
probably still unrealistic.

I don't want you to feel like a failure; I want you to experience some
victories in every area of your life so that you know you can do whatever
God is calling you to. Besides, we know there is perfection only in Jesus.
Anything we try to make perfect on our own just leads to anger, frustration, and (for Martha Stewart, the queen of perfection) jail time.

So what is one area where you could reset some standards in your

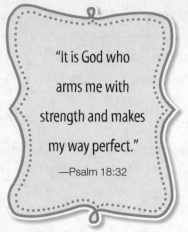

"It is God who arms me with strength and makes my way perfect."

—Psalm 18:32

life? Is it cutting back on overtime at work? Cutting down from having your daughter in three different dance classes to just two? Letting the kids fold their own clothes (imperfectly)?

Much of the time, our feelings of inadequacy come from the expectations of others. I have gotten into a lot of trouble by trying to please everyone around me instead of following my own imperfect path.

And for most of us? The worst taskmaster, the most unreasonable person with the most out-of-whack expectations, is ourselves.

Look at what my friend Ann had to say about her battle with perfectionism:

"If you can't do it right, don't do it at all." My grandfather said that when I was less than 10 years old. I was sweeping the driveway to help clean the garage.

Oosh! Little did I know that the seed of perfectionism planted so early in my life would stay with me so long. I tend to want to do everything really well, an all-or-nothing person. I still struggle with the notion that my house doesn't have to be perfect for company. Typically I am overwhelmed with housecleaning because it's just too much to keep it perfect, so I tend to let it go to the backburner. Someone said to me, "If you found out Mother Teresa had a messy house, would that change how you view her good deeds or her as a person?" When I almost answered yes, I realized I had some work to do on myself.

Lately I have learned to let go of the perfectionism, to listen to what my husband and kids really need instead of what I want. My daughter wants play dates at our house. OK, let's get the house picked up, but don't stress about the overhead dusting. She and her friends are only six years old!

My struggle with perfectionism really came into focus one Sunday morning. One portion from that morning's sermon jumped out at me: "If I could give you one thing, it would be that you could see yourself as God sees you. Our loving, forgiving Father would not, I suppose, say some of the things we say to ourselves: stupid, ugly, lazy. Only when we have the love of God and experience the love He has for us by forgiving and loving ourselves, not in a narcissistic way, can we truly love our brothers and sisters as Jesus taught us."

I'm not sure why at that moment those words sank in and had profound meaning for me. (Perhaps it was because the kids were sick and weren't with me so I could actually hear what was being said!) To love myself unconditionally the way I love my own children seemed so foreign yet so simple.

Am I still a perfectionist? Yes, I still have those urges to lift the burner pans and clean under the stove each night even though no one can see under there. The difference is now I can say, it's OK to play tag in the house with my kids and forgive myself for leaving a pan on the stove a little while longer. I can focus on the things that are truly important, instead of responding to the unreasonable—and ungodly—self-talk from before.

The Not-To-Do List

For today I would like for you to first pray about and then write out your Not-To-Do List. A Not-To-Do List is a list of those things you could give up—or do a little less perfectly—to lower some of your expectations for yourself.

I know the first thing many women are going to write on this list is "Give up 30 minutes of TV." I understand. I love a good *Gilmore Girls* rerun as much as the next girl.

But I want you to go a bit deeper. Do you always make homemade snacks to take to your Bible study because you want the recognition? Instead, buy some cheese and crackers as you're shopping for groceries the Tuesday before.

I have a friend who vacuumed the entire house every day. She lived for those lines in the carpet. When she told me she didn't have time to go to a class she had wanted to take, I challenged her to vacuum only three times a week. (Actually, it was a vacuuming intervention by me and three of her other friends.) After a lot of resistance, she was able to get down to four times a week—and take her class.

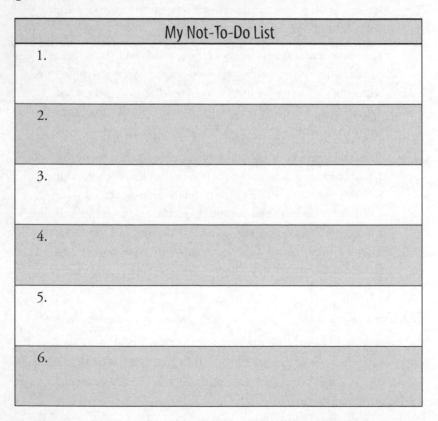

My Not-To-Do List
1.
2.
3.
4.
5.
6.

Prayer for Today

God, let me settle for nothing less than Your perfect will, and let me strive for nothing more than what is important to You.

Getting Creative

- If you are having a hard time coming up with anything for your Not-To-Do List, ask a friend who has your best interests at heart. It may not be such a great idea to ask a husband or child for this kind of input.

- When I complained about not having enough time at work, my supervisor put me on a time study to track how I was using my time. It became obvious very quickly that I was spending a lot of time working to perfection on the reports my boss was going to see, and less time on the actual work. It may be valuable to do a time study for a day or even a couple of days. All you do is set an alarm on your watch or phone for every 15 minutes, and then write down what you are doing at that time. You may be amazed at the amount of time you spend on things that just aren't that important to you.

Project Reports

"For me it's not a matter of giving up something; rather, it's giving myself freedom to pursue my activity. I'm always feeling a half step behind with the household chores or my Bible study homework. The reality is there's enough time for it all. I probably waste at least 15 minutes procrastinating and debating which activity deserves my attention more. So, if I must give up something, then it should be that time-robbing demon, *procrastination*."—Patty

Your Plan for the Project *(copy your plan on* The Me Project *Planner at the back of this book)*

Results

Who Are You Listening To?
Deciding What Goes into Your Brain

*"The right to be heard does not automatically
include the right to be taken seriously."*

Hubert Humphrey

Your Project

Think long and hard about the messages you are letting into
your mind. Is there a negative person in your life that you need
to establish better boundaries with? Are you giving yourself
bad messages? Take a step to create those boundaries today.

Tossing the 8-Tracks (Getting Rid of Old Tapes)

I have struggled with weight all my life. I go up, I go down. It's nice
to know that when I get to heaven I will have a perfect body, but for
now, I still have to shop in the women's section of actual department
stores.

For the most part, my friends and family are an incredible support to me and love me through my struggle. They lovingly hold me
accountable when I'm working hard at controlling my food and exercise, and gently encourage me back to health when I'm slacking off. I
am blessed to be surrounded by such safe and sane people.

But every group has that one person. You know who I'm talking
about. She may call herself "a truth teller," or perhaps she's just blunt
beyond what's socially acceptable. Maybe you just call her mean.

After I had my first baby, I was talking with a group of women and said offhandedly, "Yep, time to get back to the gym. I need to lose this baby weight" (and then some).

One of my relatives (her name has been withheld to protect the stupid) looked at me and said, "You know, it's going to be harder to lose the weight now that you had a baby."

I burned inside. Hurt and angry, I thought to myself (but didn't have the guts to say), *Really! Oh, thanks so much for sharing with me! I think you've missed your calling as a motivational speaker.*

I would love to say that I just brushed that comment aside, but that baby is now in college, and I remember that person's comment like it was last week's episode of *Project Runway*.

We all have those things that were said to us or about us that stick with us.

- "Really? You're trying out for choir? Don't you have to be able to sing to be in choir?"

- "I thought you were smarter than that." (Actually said to my husband by a coworker.)

- "It might be easier to work out if you lost some weight." (Really? This has to be one of the craziest statements in the English language.)

Tapes from the Past

The block where I grew up in San Jose, California, was a great place for families. There were tons of kids to play with, everyone knew each other, and we lived at each other's houses. The Springers were cool because they had the pool and the teenagers all of us little kids were desperate to hang out with. We loved to hang out with the Eglands because their mom was bright and funny, just like the daughters I loved to play with, and the Dabneys? Well, their dad was a cofounder of Atari, the video-game company that invented Pong, the first arcade game (if you were born in the eighties or later, ask your mom), so they were extra cool.

So what was hip about my family? Our jungle gym. We had a very cool play structure that was barely climbed on. What we used it for, almost daily for a while, was to get married.

In our girly, elementary-school minds, that jungle gym was the perfect wedding gazebo. And it had another built-in attraction—a ready-made groom in my little brother, Brian.

Yes, all the little girls lined up to take their turns at a crack at matrimony with Brian. (An ironic side note is that as an adult, Brian didn't end up getting "State of California Legally Married" until he was 40. But when he did get married, he got a great girl!)

As we all took turns walking down the aisle, I couldn't wait for my chance to be the bride. Getting to be the center of attention? I was all over that. When it was my turn, my brother turned to me and said, "I only marry pretty girls."

Now before you ask for Brian's address to bring the pitchforks and torches on my behalf, he was five at the time he made that comment. But even though he didn't mean to say anything to hurt me, those kinds of statements can stick with a girl.

Isn't it funny how we could have 98 people tell us that we look great, did a wonderful job on that report, our kids are great, and the painting we just finished is a-*maz*-ing, but if 2 people criticize us, those are the comments that stick to our soul.

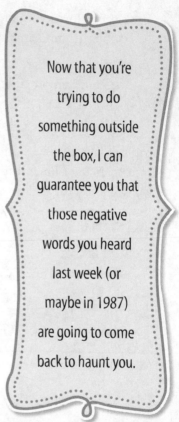

Now that you're trying to do something outside the box, I can guarantee you that those negative words you heard last week (or maybe in 1987) are going to come back to haunt you.

Now that you're trying to do something outside the box—follow God in a new or different direction, try something that you've never tried before, explore a dream or passion that you have tried to ignore— I can guarantee you that those negative words you heard last week (or maybe in 1987) are going to come back to haunt you.

Here are some of the things that may be playing in your head:

- "You're just being selfish."
- "If only you had started going to school earlier, you might have a life by now."
- "If you loved your life, that would be enough—you wouldn't need anything else."
- "Why are you spending time on yourself? You should be spending more time with your (job, friends, kids, husband, church)."

Satan is the deceiver who will use every avenue—especially a woman's guilt—to throw us off balance and steal the joy God has waiting for us by living a life fully designed by Him.

I want you to take five minutes to write down all the reasons you:

- Can't
- Shouldn't
- Have no business working on this goal.

Who Is the Voice?	What Are They Saying?	What Do I Need to Do About it?
(Me, Mom, Teacher?)		(Spend less time with them? Scripture?)

Who Is the Voice?	What Are They Saying?	What Do I Need to Do About it?

Write them all down—every excuse, every reality, every negative thought you have. Make a list, write a paragraph, write a haiku if you need to, just get it down. Because if you don't acknowledge it, you can't deal with it.

Current Tapes

My daughter Kimber and I have an ongoing discussion about the kind of music she listens to. She will sing along to my worship albums and oldies (oldies being anything from the nineties or earlier), but when she asks to control the music while she's driving, I have to steel myself.

I do love some of her music (OK, maybe *love* is too strong a word, but some of her bands I can tolerate); then, every once in a while, I will hear a word or phrase that catches my attention. "Did they just say what I think they said?" Thoughts of my daughter in Sunday school, reciting verses from Philippians, seem like a more and more distant memory.

Her argument is the same one my friends and I used (unsuccessfully) on our parents—the argument that has been used ever since Elvis Presley swiveled his hips in front of fascinated teenagers and horrified parents on the *Ed Sullivan Show*: "Really, I'm not listening to the lyrics. Just the music." Uh-huh. Right.

And the funny thing is, sometimes she doesn't recognize what they're saying, even though she knows the words by heart. It becomes a sort of mindless brainwashing.

Whether it's the kind of music we listen to on our iPod, the TV we watch, or the people we hang out with, we need to be careful about who we listen to.

It's so easy to let messages get into our heads—messages that have no business being there and are not from God.

The Crazy Folder

When I saw the e-mail with Terry's name on it, I had a decision to make. Terry (not her real name) is someone I have struggled with for years. She is smart, funny, adorable, creative, and outgoing. And I was jealous. I mean green-with-envy jealous.

Whenever our boss would get excited about her idea, I was jealous that he never seemed excited about my idea. When men would pay attention to her because of her cuteness and great personality, I was jealous. When coworkers would laugh at her jokes or give her extra attention during meetings, I was jealous.

There was just something about her that bugged me. It wasn't her looks. Some of my best friends are drop-dead gorgeous (and I still love them despite that little flaw). I thought she was funny, but I was often the target of her sometimes biting humor. And still—I wrestled with the feelings of envy.

Not very attractive on my part, I know.

Things had grown increasingly tense between Terry and me. There were jabs that hurt (on both our parts), and I needed to spend some time with God, get my attitude right, and apologize. Which I did.

But the jabs and the put-downs kept coming. After a meeting, I would get an e-mail or a phone call from Terry letting me know how I had hurt her. There would often be a list of three or four things that I had said that had offended her—after a 45-minute meeting.

It was strange. In every other area of my life, I was able to meet with people, hold down a job, volunteer at church, and work on school committees without offending people. But with Terry, there was always something.

So I tried harder not to offend her. I had a friend who was also in those meetings, listening to what I said to make sure I didn't say anything that would hurt Terry's feelings. And still the phone calls and e-mails kept coming.

The accusations became more crazy and frustrating. Things I said were taken wildly out of context, slights were inferred where none were meant, and I couldn't do a thing to appease her.

The situation became debilitating for me. I stopped talking at meetings, and I skipped them altogether when I could. I no longer volunteered for assignments. I was scared to do anything because of the repercussions that I could encounter from Terry.

And that is when I created the Crazy Folder.

The Crazy Folder is simply a folder on my e-mail program where I can put any e-mail that I probably shouldn't engage in. When I saw an e-mail from Terry, I had a decision to make. Do I open it and reengage in all the drama, or do I put it in the Crazy Folder.

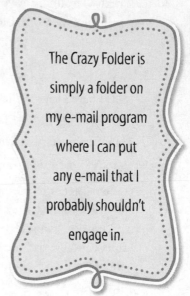

The Crazy Folder is simply a folder on my e-mail program where I can put any e-mail that I probably shouldn't engage in.

I put it in the Crazy Folder.

Once I did that, I had instant peace. Terry's actions were crazy-making for me, and I chose not to engage. Later that day, I had my husband read through the e-mail, judge that there was nothing of value in it, and trash it.

Let me be the first to say that I ask for—and get—regular feedback. I have some brutally honest friends who will tell me the truth—in love. I have editors and agents, publicists and an advisory board. I have a husband and kids who all let me know when I need to rethink how I'm doing something. I have no shortage of truth-tellers in my life.

Then there are people who just want to be hateful—people who apparently have no bigger delight than to get me off track from what God is bringing out in my life. And if I listen to them instead of to

God and the people He is using to speak into my life, I am going to be
in for a world of hurt.

Some people will even use God's Word against you, saying that pursuing anything for yourself is outside God's will for your life (even if
they have no idea whether God planted that dream for you).

In the midst of this whole Terry drama, I ran across the following
blog posting from Pastor Steven Furtick of Elevation Church in Char-
lotte, North Carolina. I love his approach to being intentional about
letting only what is profitable reach his desk:

"No mo' Technorati"

It was wrong and I knew it.

See, I have a strict policy about not reading the negative critical emails that come in around here.

"How many negative critical emails do you get?"

I don't know. I told you, I don't read them.

All emails sent to me are screened. The constructive, helpful
stuff that you send in is delivered straight to me in a nice little
stack every Wednesday. Sometimes I read those emails 2 or 3
times, and I rejoice. And I'm humbled. I write in my journal
and thank God that He would use someone like me to encourage others. God is good and gracious, and I thank Him.

The stuff that isn't constructive and encouraging is sorted, and
either handled by another staff member, or deleted, which-
ever is appropriate.

For example: An email calling me cocky and arrogant would
get deleted, probably before even being read in its entirety.

An email with an honest question about what we believe based
on something I said with a positive tone would be followed
up with.

I know 3 or 4 of you (and it's always just 3 or 4. Thousands
of people read this blog every month, dozens send in encouragement, and the 3 or 4 that don't like it are the ones that

would stick to my soul, if I read them. Isn't that stupid? That's why I don't read them.) are thinking one or more of the following things:

1. You shouldn't isolate yourself from all negative feedback.

I don't. My wife, my lead staff, and my mentors get to tell me whatever they need to tell me in appropriate settings. They know me and love me. I listen to them. Ask them and they'll verify.

I also spend an hour with a professional counselor every week, I have 2 "accountability partners" (if that's what you like to call them), and my sermons under-go a weekly voluntary critique from a trusted friend at another church.

That's not being isolated, friend. That's being intentional.

2. You don't even have the guts to respond to your critics.

I do have the guts. I just don't have the time. Or the desire.

3. Aren't you setting yourself up as untouchable?

No. I'm setting myself up to last in ministry for the long haul. The number one reason pastors leave the ministry is discouragement. By committing myself to the practice of selective hearing, I'm building in parameters for protection.

If everybody with an email account and an opinion had unfiltered access to me, it wouldn't make me more humble.

It would make me focused on what others think more than what Jesus thinks.

That's the epitome of pride, and the antithesis of humility. And I refuse to be a slave to the fear of man.

However, I'm ashamed to say that recently I found a loophole in my own system.

It's called Technorati. The way I understand it, it's a search engine for blogs. I do know that it allows me to see what others are saying about me and my blog with up to the hour accuracy.

I got addicted to it 2 weeks ago. Today my detox begins.

I refuse to ride the roller coaster.

For every 10 guys with blogs who think I'm a hero, another guy thinks I'm the anti-Christ.

And the more God elevates the influence of Elevation, the more dangerous and nauseating the roller coaster will become. So I've decided to bail.

Lori, Chunks, Larry, and Damion will continue to keep up with this stuff. That's their job.

And they'll show me the stuff I need to see. Who's reading and what they're saying, when it's appropriate.

The encouraging stuff will safely arrive on my desk regularly. And I'll rejoice.

Not because I'm an ego maniac who needs to receive praise. But because when I know God has used me to help you, it causes me to praise Him.

I'm in the ministry to help people and change lives. When that is happening, I've got to know. It fuels my fire to stay in the fight.

I'll let Jesus and those who know my heart inform my perspective of who I am and how I'm doing…

Not every college student living in his mom's basement with a blogspot and a cable modem.

If you don't like this approach or philosophy, feel free to blog about it.

As of today, I'll never know…

A couple of my pastor friends who read this blog need to be set free too.

You know who you are. Let these verses sink deep into your spirit:

"This is a trustworthy saying. And I want you to stress these things, so that those who have trusted in God may be careful to devote themselves to doing what is good. These things are excellent and profitable for everyone.

"But avoid foolish controversies and genealogies and arguments and quarrels about the law, because these are unprofitable and useless. Warn a divisive person once, and then warn him a second time. After that, have nothing to do with him" (Titus 3:8-10).

(Steven Furtick, "No mo' Technorati," March 19, 2007, http://www.stevenfurtick.com/elevation/no-mo%e2%80%99-technorati/ Used by permission.)

I love that: Avoid foolish controversies. Whether it is someone who thinks they know God's will for your life, someone who is stirring the pot for no apparent reason, or someone who just loves to fight, remember to ask, is it "unprofitable and useless"?

Be careful who you listen to.

Prayer for Today

Dear God, I pray that the voice I hear most clearly every day is Yours.

Getting Creative

- Make sure you are keeping the right company. Limit your time with people who are discouraging or negative. I know it can be hard to put limits on those relationships, but you do have some control over how people treat you.

- If you are the one giving yourself negative tapes, it's time to start viewing yourself through God's eyes instead of your own broken, distorted mirror. Meditate on Scripture that combats the wrong thinking you have going on. Here are some that have been important to me:

"The thief comes only to steal and kill and destroy; I have come that they may have life, and have it to the full" (John 10:10).

"However, as it is written:
'No eye has seen,
no ear has heard,
no mind has conceived
what God has prepared for those who love him.'"
(1 Corinthians 2:9)

"For God so loved the world that he gave his one and only Son, that whoever believes in him shall not perish but have eternal life" (John 3:16).

"But God demonstrates his own love for us in this: While we were still sinners, Christ died for us" (Romans 5:8).

"The LORD appeared to us in the past, saying:
'I have loved you with an everlasting love;
I have drawn you with loving-kindness.'"
(Jeremiah 31:3)

Project Reports

"I was in a physically and verbally abusive relationship for many years. More than the physical pain was the verbal abuse that I endured. The tapes run through my mind from time to time.

"How do I let those go? It's been years, and they still pop up from time to time. I have to pray specifically to let them go. I am a new person. Even if all those tapes were true (which they are not) I am still a new person through Christ!

"The awesomeness of God is that through Him I am worthy of the life He has blessed me with. God has blessed me with a wonderful man—who appreciates, supports, and encourages me. And I am thankful for that."—Penny

"I married at the end of my junior year in high school. (Not for the usual reason to marry so young. It just seemed the thing to do.) I returned to school at a new location, made friends, and did well until I was tempted away with the prospect of a job. Making money for our new life seemed better at the time, so I went for it. This failure to finish would follow me to this day.

"I have continued to learn through formal and self-education. Most would not know that I don't have a high-school diploma and actually assume that I'm a college graduate. It is I who knows the failure that sometimes makes me feel inadequate and occasionally second-guessing myself. At these times, I have to remember my successes. I am a good writer. I am an effective teacher despite the voice in my head. God is replacing my negative self-talk with a more positive version of my life. He is the great encourager, and I am constantly catching a glimpse of Him cheering me on."—Patty

"When I was a freshman in college, I was walking past the boy's dormitory, and several boys started barking at me. It has always stuck with me, because I have never thought of myself as attractive. Their barking at me confirmed my belief that I was ugly. Even as I was recalling that memory, it brought me to tears.

"I tried to find a Bible passage to combat the negative self-talk that it brings up in me. All I could come up with that added any salve to the wound was Psalm 139:14—'I praise you because I am fearfully and wonderfully made; your works are wonderful, I know that full well.'"—Kay

Your Plan for the Project *(copy your plan on* The Me Project *Planner at the back of this book)*

Results

Project 4

Pixie Cuts and Other Bad Decisions
Embracing Your Past

"Take chances, make mistakes. That's how you grow.
Pain nourishes your courage.
You have to fail in order to practice being brave."

MARY TYLER MOORE

Your Project

Think about one of the mistakes you have made in the past, and then write down what lessons you have learned from it in the space provided under the heading Getting Creative on page 81.

I can look back on several of my school pictures from the seventies and eighties with mild affection and tenderness. There is the senior picture taken 14 hours after I returned from a two-month missions trip aboard a boat floating on the English canals (two months with no hair product = one very scary senior picture). Then there's the snap of me wearing a rainbow shirt in fifth grade. With a unicorn. Under a satin jacket. Have mercy.

But my most regrettable—and memorable—photo was my fourth-grade portrait. No one told me that for a redhead with buckteeth and a green corduroy jumper, getting a bowl haircut may just push her over the edge to resemble the guy on the Lucky Charms box.

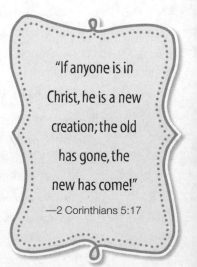

"If anyone is in Christ, he is a new creation; the old has gone, the new has come!"

—2 Corinthians 5:17

You see, before there was the Jennifer or even the Farrah, there was the Dorothy—Dorothy Hamill that is. Dorothy Hamill was the Olympic ice skater of the seventies. She won gold at the 1976 Olympics and won the hearts of the world. She has always been ranked as one of the most likable athletes in sports. But her most lasting legacy will always remain the bad school portraits that I and so many other children of the seventies ended up with.

"The Dorothy" was kindly called a wedge cut—but for most of us it would have been just as easy to set a Tupperware mixing bowl on our heads and let our little brothers hack at our hair with a pair of hedge trimmers. Yes, it was that bad.

My mom couldn't talk me out of it. I'd made up my mind—and now I live with the consequences every time I sort through old pictures.

What did I learn from that experience? The lessons were many:

1. Just because a haircut is popular doesn't mean it's going to work on you.

2. Redheads with gaps in their teeth that a VW Bug could drive through should not have a haircut that hits at the tooth line.

3. I need to treat the goofy red-headed kid of my youth with a lot of tenderness. It was not easy growing up knowing that I was one of the funniest-looking kids in school. My older self can be a lot kinder to my younger self when I remember what it was like to be the chubby, bowl-cut girl.

4. The smartest, most interesting people were absolutely tortured in elementary school. I wish that the formative years for every child were warm and embracing, but for most of us, they are not. It's a little less *High School Musical* and a little more *Lord of the Flies*. But I also know that some of those experiences have given me an extra measure of compassion and tenderness toward those who don't quite fit the mold.

You have probably made some mistakes—maybe even some big ones. Mistakes that have taken you off course and made you feel like a total failure. Besides bowl cuts, I have had some doozies:

- Getting pregnant before I was married

- Not finishing college

- A failed first marriage

Mistakes are hard and painful. Most of us will do anything we can to avoid making them.

Every woman I know has regrets from some area of her life, whether it's decisions she made or decisions that were made for her. Maybe it was not continuing school, poor choices in a relationship, hanging out with people who were not making good choices, bad career decisions, being irresponsible with our parenting. The list goes on and on.

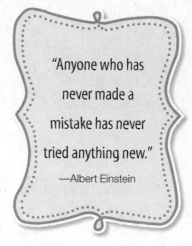

"Anyone who has never made a mistake has never tried anything new."

—Albert Einstein

But what is often more tragic than making mistakes is the woman who will not learn from them.

Learning from Our Mistakes

Too often women make the same mistake over and over, and instead of changing what they're doing, they spend all their time making excuses about why things can never change.

I am not going to stop making mistakes. I am still going to make some big hairy ones. My hope is they will be different big hairy mistakes than the ones I've made before. Because as much as I would love to believe that I can behave my way into perfection, stepping carefully through life, never touching my toe outside the boundary lines, that is not my reality.

My reality is that any wisdom I have gained, any progress I've made

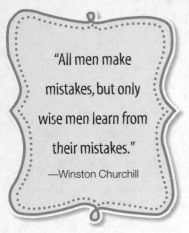

"All men make mistakes, but only wise men learn from their mistakes."

—Winston Churchill

in becoming more Christlike than I was five years ago, is because of the mistakes I've made and God's lessons through the pain.

I never learn anything through good circumstances. I learn only through pain. I wish it were different. I wish that I learned my lessons while singing worship songs or eating Godiva Chocolates or shopping. But sadly, that's not how I roll.

I learn when I hurt someone with the words that I've said when I see the pain on their face. And yet, the point is to learn.

Look at how my friend Miriam learned from an e-mail that she knows she never should have sent:

When the new president took office, one of the very first decisions he made is one that I vehemently disagreed with. I immediately sent out a very sarcastic e-mail voicing my dissatisfaction over this to many of my friends and family that I assumed would sympathize with my frustration. One friend and one family member were quite offended by my e-mail, so much so that I had to send another e-mail out apologizing to everyone and telling them what I learned from this experience. That was:

1. Never assume that just because someone is a fellow believer in Christ, she/he sees the world in the same way that I do.

2. Sarcasm never makes a situation better.

3. E-mail is the worst possible way to express dissatisfaction to a group of people over anything.

4. When faced with a problem that I cannot myself change, the best thing to do is pray and ask the only one who can

change it to let God's will reign, not fire off a seething e-mail to much of my address book.

Being a pastor's wife, I was horribly embarrassed by this relational screw-up, and it was very humbling to have to say, "I messed up big time, please forgive me."

I thought I had ruined my relationships with my friend and relative, but afterward, they loved me even more for admitting my error and asking for public forgiveness, and our relationship is stronger now. If I had just shrunk into a hole and tried to forget this happened, I hate to think what those two people would think of me now, and how that would affect my life and ministry as a whole. I definitely learned a huge lesson from this mess up.

I love that Miriam actively looked for ways not only to correct her mistake, but also to take a life-changing lesson from it. A lesson that has not only drawn her closer to Christ, but also to the people she hurt. She was able to share her mistake with others and turn it into a teaching opportunity instead of a secret shame. Love that. God doesn't waste a thing.

Prayer for Today

Help me learn from every mistake I have made. Let me be transformed because of the correction You have lovingly given me in my life.

Getting Creative

- Still feeling guilty or discouraged from a past mistake? Write down all the things that God has taught you through it. Nothing, including those big hairy mistakes, is wasted in God's economy.

Project Reports

"I went back to finish college when I was 48 and graduated at age 50. Algebra was tough. I took it by correspondence from a Christian college. Though I knew enough to get an A, I wanted a higher A, and I cheated. Afterward, my personality changed. I knew I'd sinned, but I didn't deal with it for almost a year. I found that I did everything that year totally in the flesh. God broke my heart at a revival meeting, and I confessed to Him and wrote the school to confess too. Everyone sitting under my ministry told me that I had new freedom in my speaking after that.

"I've learned that integrity matters more than results. That is a hallmark of my ministry with women as I speak to them about the choices in their lives."—Dawn

Your Plan for the Project *(copy your plan on* The Me Project *Planner at the back of this book)*

Results

Project 5

No Small Feet
Goals That Are Custom Made for You

"Why compare yourself with others?
No one in the entire world can do a better job
of being you than you."

Author unknown

Your Project

Have you wasted time comparing yourself to other people in your life? Time to acknowledge it and move on.

It was the early nineties, and I had been living in Japan as a missionary for half a year when the situation turned desperate. I was running out of shoes.

You see, six months earlier, after weighing and reweighing my luggage for my trip to Tokyo for training, the numbers were still not adding up. I needed to get my two suitcases down to less than 50 pounds each.

I had shipped all my books and teaching materials ahead. All that was left to pack were enough clothes to get me through the year. As I sat in my bedroom surrounded by my favorite shoes, shirts, bags, and jackets, considering what accessories I needed to leave behind, I seriously started to reconsider how badly the people of Uji Baptist Church needed an English teacher. Couldn't I just send them some *Knots Landing* reruns and a *Flashdance* video? That was about all the English anyone would ever need—right?

Once I came to my senses, I started repacking for the fifth time. I tell you, it was like a scene out of *Sophie's Choice*. It was unfathomable to me that I couldn't bring both of my lime-green purses. You know, a big slouchy one for casual days walking around Kyoto and a dressier one for church and going out with friends for dinner. It made perfect sense to me.

I now know what it's like for an employer to lay off some of his favorite staff: "You have great potential. You are really a great peasant blouse, but we are going in a different direction, and you just don't fit in with the 'casual/preppy with a touch of Rachel from *Friends*' look we are going for."

The hardest decisions to make were with my shoes. I have a special relationship with my footwear. My mom is an 8½ wide and my dad wears a 14 AAA. My feet are about the same size of those of the love child of Wilt Chamberlain and Sasquatch. I wear a size 11.

If you're having trouble picturing what a size 11 women's shoe looks like, go grab the skateboard your next-door neighbor's son leaves on your driveway every night. OK, now imagine that in the size of a shoe—that's approximately the size of the strappy slingback I am on the hunt for every time I hit the department stores.

Leaving shoes behind was heartbreaking but necessary. I whittled my selection down to six pairs. After saying goodbye to all those faithful soles who were left behind, I packed up my precious six and headed for the mission field.

Now I know that being a missionary in Japan brings about the same connotation as being a lifeguard in Honolulu. While I was still working hard I wasn't exactly roughing it. The biggest difference in my day-to-day life was that in the U.S., as a typical 22-year-old, I drove everywhere. If I were going to the supermarket 1.5 blocks away, I took my car. In Japan, I walked everywhere. Then, after getting home, I climbed four flights of stairs to get to my tiny apartment on the top floor.

While I was developing "Calves of Steel," I was also developing holes in my shoes. My babies were falling apart.

The situation was becoming desperate. If I thought buying shoes in the States was hard, finding anything in Japan large enough to cover the feet that God (and my dad) gave me was impossible. Too broke to go to the repair shop, I resorted to wearing cardboard in the bottom of my shoes. I limped along—literally—like that for weeks, before she came into my life.

I had heard a rumor that she was out there. Another missionary from the States who was as addicted to footwear as I was. She was from New York. She had lived in Japan for years. She was a size 11.

Her name was Dawn, and without even meeting her, I didn't like her. I was jealous—and curious. How did someone who lived in Japan and wore a size 11 have such an array of great shoes?

The first night I met her was at a party in the tiny apartment she shared with one of my friends. I was desperate to meet her, and equally desperate to see her shoe collection.

For someone I didn't know and that I had spent a great deal of time wishing a foot ailment on (that way, she'd have to wear orthopedics and give away her extensive foot wardrobe), Dawn could not have been nicer. She graciously welcomed me into her home and introduced me to all her friends. She had prepared a lovely dinner for all of us to share.

After containing myself for several whole minutes, I couldn't help but blurt out, "Can I see your shoes?"

She took me to her closet and, like Toto pulling back the curtain on the Wizard of Oz, revealed where all the magic was. Her shoes were beautiful. They sat in a jumble on the closet like a crazy fruit salad. Blues and greens, canary yellow…every color you could imagine. I just stood there with my mouth hanging open.

And then she said the words that would change my life.

"You wear a size 11? Well, if you ever want to borrow some, you totally can."

That was the beginning of a beautiful relationship. I would go over and visit her shoes (and her) about once a week, returning the pair I had borrowed and picking up another pair for the coming week. To thank her, I always brought a pan of brownies.

One week I borrowed a pair of brown sandals that were the most

beautiful chocolate-colored leather, buttery soft—little works of art. I
had seen Dawn wear them several times, and I had just fallen in love

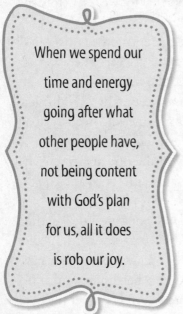

with them. I was so excited when I finally
got to bring them home for a visit.

That Tuesday, I left my apartment
wearing the beautiful sandals for my once-
a-week trip to Osaka, which involved several train trips and a great deal of walking
up and down hills. I was so glad to have
the sandals.

Until the pain started.

After walking about six blocks, the
leather started rubbing on the sides of my
feet. After another two blocks, rubbing on
turned into digging into. Once I got to
the first train station, I could barely walk.

The rest of the day I was miserable.
Every step I took caused more pain. How
could those beautiful sandals have turned
into such instruments of torture?

When we spend our time and energy going after what other people have, not being content with God's plan for us, all it does is rob our joy.

I returned the sandals to Dawn, assuring her that she would never
have to worry about me borrowing that pair of shoes again. I told her
the story of my sore feet and how surprised I was that the shoes were
such a poor fit.

She smacked her hand against her head and said, "Oh, that's right.
Those are the sandals I had made for me. They're a custom fit. I bet they
did hurt. I am so sorry."

Trying to walk around in shoes that were custom made for someone else is a lot like trying to live a life that God custom designed for
someone else. It may look pretty on the outside for a little while, but
all it will bring is frustration, misery, and pain.

I spend so much time wanting what other people have, seeing what
my friends' lives are like and wanting their circumstances to be my
circumstances.

God has a life that is custom designed for each of us. When we spend our time and energy going after what other people have, not being content with God's plan for us, all it does is rob our joy.

Today, I want you to spend some time thinking, really thinking, about those people you may be envious of or comparing yourself to. We all do it—a lot. The problem comes when we don't recognize it and combat it.

We have to be assured that God has not made a mistake with the gifts and talents He has given specifically to us. Comparing is a waste of energy and a waste of the purpose God has uniquely given us to accomplish.

Spend some time right now and look at all the people you are comparing yourself to. Write down their names and the gifts they have that you want. If you feel safer doing this on a separate piece of paper, and then destroying the paper, that's a fine way to go.

When I struggle with jealousy, I eventually realize that it's not really about the other person. It's usually about my own fear of either A) not accomplishing what I think God wants me to accomplish, or B) being off track in my understanding of God's will.

Here is a verse that I hang on my mirror (and put on my desktop and clip to my car's visor) when I am dealing with jealousy:

> "Each one should test his own actions. Then he can take pride in himself, without comparing himself to somebody else, for each one should carry his own load" (Galatians 6:4-5).

Prayer for Today

God, I know that comparing myself to other people does not come from You. I pray that I would start to see myself only through Your eyes.

Getting Creative

- Jealousy breeds when we are ignorant of the other person's circumstances. Jealous of that friend that's an overnight

success? What you may not know is that she has been
working on her craft for over ten years without success.
Get to know the person and her story.

- Knowing that God has a specific, different plan for your
  life is very freeing. Make sure you feel confident in knowing God's plan for you (reviewing Project 1 could be a
  place to start).

Project Reports

"When I first started speaking, I felt I had to constantly give
churches the disclaimer: 'I'm no Beth Moore.' I was so self-
conscious that the enemy jumped on that thought and grew it
to a fear that discouraged me to tears the week before I would
speak. The Lord used Psalm 138:7-8 to show me I was the
work of His hands, He loved me, and would stretch forth His
hand against the wrath of my enemy. Today, the enemy still
tries, but my confidence and speaking ability is from the Lord.
It is He who speaks through me and not myself. Lest I would
boast."—Mimi

Your Plan for the Project *(copy your plan on* The Me Project *Planner
at the back of this book)*

Results

Dumbo's Flying Lesson
Figuring Out What You Don't Need

"Just do it."

NIKE SLOGAN

Your Project

What excuses are you making that are causing you to not accomplish your goal? Acknowledge them, write them down, and then make a plan to combat them with truth.

Do You Spend All Your Time Saddling Up?

I once heard about a speaker who was talking to a group of employees about efficiency. During one of the breaks, one of the employees came up and started to show the guest speaker the organizational system he used. He had all the bells and whistles that any cell phone/PDA could contain—a calendar (with minute-by-minute reminders), to-do lists, integrated systems with his laptop and home and work computers, work flowcharts, and productivity tools. After the show and tell, the guest speaker was chatting with some of the guys' coworkers. When she commented on what an elaborate system was contained in that small cell phone, the other employees rolled their eyes and said, "Yeah, but he spends all his time working on the system and never gets any real work done. It's like he spends all his time saddling up, but the horse never moves."

For a long time, I was that way with writing. I figured I would start to *really* write after I had taken a class for *real* writers. Or I would start to write when I had the right book to tell me what to do. I would get serious about writing once I wasn't working full-time or the kids were in school. Then it became when the kids were out of school, then when the kids were grown—that would be the perfect time to write.

This crazy thinking manifested itself in a lot of procrastination and excuses. There was the location. Oh, the back porch would be the perfect place to write—once the weather got better. In the meantime, I would need to write in my bedroom office, which would be perfect if I could just clean up that area to give me some space. So instead of writing, I would clean. In the midst of cleaning, I would pick up a bill that needed to be paid or an article I had been meaning to read and log on to my computer to pay the bill or grab a Diet Coke and sit down to read the article.

And I wondered why I could never get anything written.

I kept waiting for the perfect time to write. In my little fantasy, I was in a cabin somewhere in the woods, with meal delivery and no wireless Internet to distract me. Funny, no one was offering a cozy little cabin for me to write in.

When I finally succumbed to the fact that no set of circumstances was going to magically make the words flow more easily, I decided perfect had to go out the window, to be replaced with writing in my minivan 15 minutes before picking up kids from school.

Dumbo's Feather and Why You Are Not Getting It Done

Remember the Disney movie *Dumbo*? When his friend and mentor, Timothy, discovers himself and Dumbo up in a tree, he convinces Dumbo that the way he could fly is with the help of a magic feather. As long as he held the feather in his trunk, he could avoid crashing to the ground and thrill the circus audience. But Dumbo was convinced that as soon as he lost his feather, he would lose the ability to fly.

I was like Dumbo. If I didn't have the perfect circumstances—if I didn't sit in the right coffee shop, have the perfect idea, have complete quiet (or the right songs on my iPod), have my kids in school, have the kitchen clean—I couldn't work toward my dream of becoming a writer.

My son Justen is also a writer, but he actually writes. He writes during breaks from school. He writes at the coffee shop downtown. He writes before going to bed and when he first gets up in the morning. He writes for college classes and when he should be doing other things. ("Justen! Stop writing and listen to the sermon. I'm testing you on the way home!") Justen could come up with a million reasons not to write. But he writes.

If I wait until things are perfect, I am never going to make any progress.

When we are looking to live the life God designed for us, we often wait for "the big gift" from God to make it all possible. Before you start even thinking about opening that small business you've always dreamed of, maybe you're waiting for the money to buy the equipment you need, the time to go to school full-time, or for your kids to get older. You don't know when the time is going to be *right*, but you know that it isn't *right now*.

When I asked some of my Facebook friends what was keeping them from living out their God-given dreams, the number one answer was "Stage of life." The funny thing is, the women who responded were from every stage of life: stay-at-home moms, working single women, grandmothers, and retirees. Many of the women seemed to assume that life was going to change for the better and that at some point in the future, things would settle down.

It's just another form of the magic feather.

If I wait until things are perfect, I am never going to make any progress. My situation is never going to be perfect.

I think perfection is just another form of fear. Fear about things not turning out. Fear of becoming overwhelmed. Fear of wasting money and energy and our time and our family's time.

Goals are never perfect and are often very, very messy. The steps don't come in 1-2-3s. I know that most people who are living some version of their dreams didn't wait for things to change; they cobbled together the resources they already had and made the best out of less-than-best circumstances.

Prayer for Today

I pray that I can see everything You have given me—every skill, every tool, every person that I need to accomplish what You want me to do.

Getting Creative

- How about giving yourself some extra incentive for just getting started—a trip to Starbucks if you spend 15 minutes making phone calls, watching a DVD if you do an hour of research on your topic. Something, anything, to get you started.

- When my daughter was looking for a new job, I told her that I would get her a new pair of jeans as soon as she got 20 rejections. Sometimes we focus on the outcome instead of the process.

Project Reports

"For the first time in my life, I'm not waiting. I'm determined to lose these pounds and none of my excuses will hold up. I used to say I didn't have time to exercise, that I deserved a treat after a hard day, or that if I didn't spend my every spare minute with my family, I'd be a bad mom and wife. This time around I can see that none of those things are legitimate. I can attribute it only to God at work in my life, because heaven knows it's totally not like me! I'm thanking Him and leaning into His amazing grace and strength."—Linda

"I keep a list of goals I wish to achieve, and I slowly but surely check them off. I find that keeping that list helps me stay focused on what I wish to do/achieve in life. I recently checked off a goal of going to the Olympics, a goal I've had for a while, but the timing wasn't right. When I saw they would be in Vancouver, I knew that was it. Since October 2008 I've been saving and planning to go, and now I can say I did and move on to my next goal.

"Some goals can be achieved in a short period of time while others take years, but at the end of my life I want to know I did just about everything I wanted to do. To me that is a life well lived."—Ramona

Your Plan for the Project *(copy your plan on* The Me Project *Planner at the back of this book)*

Results

Speeding Tickets and Other Gifts from God

Paying Attention to the Warnings Along the Way

"Pay attention and listen to the sayings of the wise;
apply your heart to what I teach,
for it is pleasing when you keep them in your heart
and have all of them ready on your lips."
PROVERBS 22:17-18

Your Project

As you work toward and pray about your goal, pay extra attention to what God is saying to you about this area of your life. Write down any direction you get.

It had been one of those mornings where, if I didn't have kids who would have destroyed the house, I would have just stayed in bed.

I'd had a fight with my husband the night before, and we still were not on speaking terms. The oatmeal cookies I baked for that morning's Bible study and left cooling on the counter were mysteriously gone, and Einstein, our golden retriever, had a combined look of satisfaction and guilt.

My daughter Kimberly was in her exhibitionist phase, and I patiently had to tell her that no, she would not be wearing a bikini top to Bible study.

I was stressed, I was frustrated, and I was late. And now I had to stop at the store to pick up replacement cookies—in the rain. Let me tell you, I was in no mood to get my Jesus on in Bible study that morning.

After stopping at the store, unloading everyone out of the car, buying the cookies, and loading both kids back into the car, I wasn't just late, I was interrupt-the-entire-Bible-study late.

As I raced toward the church, I unloaded my list of problems on my friend Vikki via cell phone (this was before I realized that driving while chatting on a cell phone was not the best idea). I poured it all out to her—how nothing was going my way, how I was so frustrated, so mad, and how this day could not get any worse.

That's when I saw the police lights in my rearview mirror.

I quickly hung up with Vikki and tried to figure out how I was going to get out of this ticket. Flirting? That may work for 20-somethings coming back from the gym, but I doubted that it was going to work for this 30-something going to Bible study with two kids in the back seat.

Denial? I knew that I was going over the speed limit, and apparently, so did his speed gun. Next.

Crying? Hey, I was on the verge anyway. Might as well give it a shot.

As the police officer approached the car, I tried to get the waterworks going, but for the first time in my adult life, I couldn't cry.

Great. Another failure. This was, officially, the worst morning of my life.

"License and registration please."

I rummaged through my glove box and my shoulder bag. It took me several minutes to find the documents, and when I finally handed them to the officer, I saw that he was already writing out the ticket. Perfect. More things to fight about with my husband when I got home.

He took both pieces of ID and copied the information onto his pad, then handed them back to me and said, "Ma'am, you were going 47 miles per hour in a 35 zone. Today is the first day of rain we've seen in a long time, and the roads are more slippery than normal. I'm not giving you a ticket, but this is a warning because I could see that you had two beautiful kids in the car, and I know that neither of us would want to see anything happen to them."

He handed me the warning, gave a quick wave to Justen and Kim in the back seat, got back in his cruiser, and pulled away.

That was more than ten years ago, but I will never forget the impact of what that officer did. If he had given me a ticket, it would have been just another item in a long list of really annoying things to happen that day. But because he gave me a

It's easy to skip over the warnings we get.

warning, along with showing how much he cared about my kids and me, to this day it has had an effect on almost every area of my life.

That warning really did make me stop and think about how out of whack I was about getting to Bible study on time. I was trying to impress women and look as if I had it all together, when the best thing I could have done was take a deep breath, say a prayer, and drive carefully to where I needed to go—with or without cookies.

It's easy to skip over the warnings we get. That officer pulling me over was annoying and an interruption to my day, but if I had not paid attention to what he said, who knows the problems I could have caused by being reckless with my speed, on my cell phone, with my kids in the car.

How do you look at the interruptions and warnings that come into your life?

- A chest pain that won't go away

- Counsel from a friend about not hanging out with a certain group of people

- That nudge (women's intuition? the Holy Spirit?) that lets you know that things are not as they seem

Recently, the warnings have been coming up again in my life. Last week I was rushing to get to a meeting at my pastor's house. I was running about five minutes late, but Roger and I had done some switching around so that I could get to this meeting closer to on time.

When I got to Scott's house, he greeted me at the door and said, "Wow, you're here with time to spare."

"I know, I know, I'm usually late, but I'm not *so* late tonight!" I said.

Then I looked around. Scott normally has snacks laid out for us when we come over. He's passing out handouts and getting the meeting kicked off. Tonight, he and his family were watching the news.

"Kathi, it's six," Scott said. "The meeting starts at seven."

Oops.

It has been a week like that for me. Going to pick my son up at school, and then remembering that he had a ride home with a friend. Leaving my debit card at a restaurant and having to drive back across town to get it. Going to the supermarket to get milk and bread, then spending $150, coming home, and realizing that I forgot the milk and bread.

Do you constantly feel discouraged and off track? Do you feel as if you've got a bunch of stumbling blocks in the road? Do you feel as though every time you get started on your goal, something or someone comes along to mess it up?

Pay attention to those warnings. God may have a message for you:

- Spend more time with Me.

- You think you know the route I want you to take, but you need to listen more closely.

- Right now is a time to wait.

- This is part of the plan. I need you to go through this to get stronger.

All I want you to do is pay attention to the warning signs. Write them down in the space below and pray about them. Ask God for direction if you are unclear whether to proceed or wait.

Warning signs God might be using to get my attention:

Prayer for Today

God, let me pay attention to the warnings You have given me. Help me recognize the Holy Spirit's work in my life and on my behalf.

Getting Creative

- Sometimes it's easier to recognize the warning signs in someone else's life. Ask a trusted friend if she sees something in your life that is out of balance. (Only ask someone who will tell you the truth—in love.)

- Is there a warning that God has been putting in your life over and over? What is the resistance to heeding that warning? Ask a friend or two to be praying with you about that rebellion and how it's showing up in your life.

Project Reports

"Around the same time I became a Christian, I got a job with a start-up computer/telephone cabling company that was growing by leaps and bounds. I was making great money. I was also working for a company full of workaholics, and I caught the disease. So much so I almost lost my family and my good health because of it. Everything suffered—family dinners around the table (I often got in from work about an hour after my family had finished), my health. Due to the added stress in my life, I had a heart attack at age 46. What an eye opener that was! After a four-month disability rest from work, I went back and realized I just couldn't do it anymore.

"As expected God provided! I was asked if I would be interested in taking a teaching position at our church's Christian academy. I wanted out from my current job, but I also looked at the tremendous cut in pay I would be receiving. After much thought and prayer, I took the position, and God has been so faithful! He has provided, and my health, family situation, and ministry have improved tremendously. My priorities have changed. I have to look at things every day from God's perspective, not my own. I certainly cannot do life without my Lord and Savior!"—Cheryl

Your Plan for the Project (*copy your plan on* The Me Project *Planner at the back of this book*)

Results

Week Two Projects

Project 8

No Deposit, No Return
Keeping Strong

"The chains of habit are generally too small to be felt
until they are too strong to be broken."
SAMUEL JOHNSON

Your Project

If you are feeling overwhelmed in taking even small steps
toward your goal, it may be that another area of your life is out
of whack. Today, I want you to look at some of the strength-
ening areas of your life and check to make sure that you are
taking good care of yourself.

For so many years, I felt like a terrible mom. I was embarrassed that
I did not get excited about going to my son's soccer games (this was
when he was eight and spent more time looking everywhere but at the
ball). I thought the opportunity to drop off my daughter at dance class
was a treat. It wasn't until about the fifth class that I realized many of
the other moms were staying to watch the rehearsals. I thought that
was what recitals were for.

Don't get me wrong. I love hanging out with my kids—and I count
it a small miracle that they like hanging out with me. We go to book-
stores and cafes and used record shops. Our family dinners (when we
actually all get to eat together) are filled with daily reports and lively conversation. We have one-on-one dates every couple of weeks to just hang
out and catch up on life. At this point they're not embarrassed to be seen
in public with me—but I know that could change at any moment.

But as much as I enjoy being with my kids, I feel a desperate need for time just for myself. When my Justen and Kimberly were little, that was extended bathroom breaks with the door ajar to make sure neither of them swallowed anything they shouldn't. Weekly, I would swap babysitting with another mom during the day so I could spend time reinvigorating myself. Sometimes that just meant a solo trip to the supermarket so I didn't have to say "Stop touching that!" six times every aisle.

While most of my alone time was simply getting errands done, sometimes I would sneak off to a local ministry here in the Bay Area that has a quiet room. A place just to think, pray, and be quiet. I even did a couple of quiet retreats for a structured time of praying and listening and waiting on God.

I hear so many young moms say, "There's no way I could take any time for myself—I can barely get the laundry done." It seems selfish to carve out any space in the day to meet our own needs. Taking care of ourselves seems counterintuitive to what a "good mom" does.

But take care of ourselves we must.

And this doesn't apply just to moms. If you are in a full-time job, it can become easy to get so wrapped up in projects at work that you never take time for yourself.

Take Care of Yourself Physically

Get Some Good Exercise

I hate exercise. If I could pay someone else to do it for me, I would. But I do it. I do it because one of my major goals in life is to weigh what is printed on my driver's license. I do it because I want to live long enough to see my kids make the same mistakes I made as a parent. But the main reason I do it is to give me energy throughout the day.

When I make time for the hour that it takes to get myself to the gym, work out, and come home, I feel better throughout the day. Even a 30-minute jump on the Wii is better than nothing—and it really does help. My stamina is better, my energy is better, and most of all, my attitude is better.

Most days my exercise consists of taking our puggle (pug-beagle mix), Jake, for his morning and evening walk. But even after those 20 or 30 minutes of walk, stop, let Jake sniff, my mind is clearer, I have a bit more energy, and I'm ready to focus on the task in front of me.

Make all the excuses you want—trust me, honey, I've used them all—but there is no legitimate excuse not to exercise. Even with small kids. Even with bad weather. Even with busy schedules. Gyms all over the country offer childcare. Malls have walking routes for women with strollers. It will be inconvenient, time consuming, tiring, and a pain. Do it anyway.

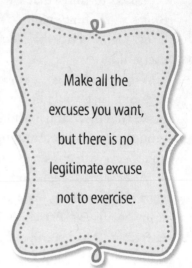

Make all the excuses you want, but there is no legitimate excuse not to exercise.

Do it because your kids love you and they want to have their mom around for a very long time.

Do it because your mom worries about your health and wants to know you are doing all you can.

Do it because your husband loves you and you want to do all those fun things later in life that you can't do right now with kids.

Do it because it takes a lot of energy to be a woman and to live out the plans and dreams God has for your life. Exercise gives you that energy.

Get Some Good Food

I've struggled with food my whole life. While I've had some great victories in this area, it still continues to be the "thorn in my flesh." I understand how hard it can be to take the time to fuel your body properly. But it is imperative for women to get the proper nutrition, not food left over from their kid's plate.

Use a blank calendar to plan out what you are going to eat for the week. That will help you to pick up foods that are healthy as you cruise the grocery store aisles. (It will also help you to avoid the typical default plan: "Oh no, it's 5:30 and I can't even think of what to eat. Golden Arches here we come…")

We are so blessed to have a bounty of fresh fruits and veggies available year-round in most parts of the country. Take advantage of this to give variety and spice to your menu.

Get Some Good Sleep

I used to think that I was an excellent sleeper—until I married Roger. Everything, and I do mean everything, affects Roger's sleep patterns. Light, noise, the pillow, the chimichanga he had for dinner—everything.

When we first got married, we took the opportunity to fashion a bedroom that would be conducive to a good night's rest. While Roger picked out the sound machine with "Ocean Waves" lulling in the background, I ordered custom blackout shades for our two big windows and sheets with obscenely high thread counts for our bed.

After our first night in our re-creation of the Stanford Sleep Clinic, something amazing happened—I woke up feeling energized. Really, really energized. "Attack the day with a bright and happy disposition" energized. It had been years since I had felt this rested.

If you are staying awake at night, and it's not because you have an 18-month-old who refuses to sleep through the night, check out your "sleep hygiene." Your sleep habits may be keeping you from getting the best night's sleep possible. Are you drinking caffeine too close to bedtime? Are you working late into the night, not giving your brain a chance to shut down? Nothing can impact your day more than the kind of sleep you got the night before. Take a good long look at your habits and make adjustments where needed. You'll thank me in the morning.

As toddlers, our kids needed rest to stay up with their active schedules and growing bodies. As women, rest is no less important with our active schedules and changing bodies. Many women wear their lack of sleep like a badge of honor. But when we get tired, it affects every part of our lives—we tend to eat more, be irritable, and it can even become dangerous. A friend from high school fell asleep at the wheel, nearly killing her husband in the ensuing accident. A lack of sleep is not something to play around with.

There has been more than one irritable afternoon when my daughter has put her arm around my shoulder and said, "I think someone needs a nap." Listen to the signals your body is sending you—and to the comments others are sending you. It may just be time for your "Time Out."

Take Care of Yourself Mentally

I remember the days of being part of a MOPS (Mothers of Pre-Schoolers) group. One day we were sitting around a table discussing our favorite musical genres, and when it was my turn to tell the group my favorite song, all I could come up with in my preschool mom's brain was a big purple dinosaur singing, "I love you, you love me, we're a happy family."

The animal may have changed, but our tendency as moms is to feed our brains a steady diet of "made for kids" media. It's easy to go through an entire day where the most mental stimulation we've had has been counting up the number of stickers on the potty chart.

Just like the good food that you put into your body, it is vital to put good media into your brain. While it may be tempting to get your grown-up time from reading about other fabulous and not-so-fabulous lives in *People* magazine, it's better to create your own fabulous life.

Surround yourself with good books and great movies. Don't have the time to read all the greats out there? Borrow books on CD to listen to in your car. The added bonus is that my kids often get as wrapped up in the stories as I do.

Some of our favorites have been biographies of great men and women we may not have been exposed to in public school. Dietrich Bonhoeffer, Corrie ten Boom, and Jim and Elisabeth Elliot were just some of the heroes that we learned more about while driving back and forth between dance lessons and chess practice. Some of our favorite stories were discovered while on long-distance road trips. *Cheaper by the Dozen* (from the classic book, not the not-so-classic Steve Martin movie), *The Prize Winner of Defiance, Ohio,* and *Marley and Me* are just a few of our favorites.

I have even listened to some CDs and podcasts related to my goals—podcasts on becoming a better speaker, CDs from writing conferences. (The rule in my car is that the driver decides what comes out of the speakers.)

Even though my kids never would have chosen to listen to those recordings, they have absorbed the information through osmosis—and we have had some great discussions about some very grown-up writing styles.

Surround yourself with good books and great movies.

Make sure that you take time to read as well. It may just be a few pages a day, but read. If you can't justify the time for yourself, remember one of your objectives as a mom is to raise a reader. Your child is much more likely to read if she catches you doing the same.

Take Care of Yourself Spiritually

When my kids were at their most high-maintenance, I was spiritually at my lowest. It felt like a luxury to put on clean clothes most mornings. The idea of having a quiet time on top of that seemed completely out of reach.

When the great reformer Martin Luther was facing an unusually busy day, he said, "I have twice as much to do today, and therefore I need to pray twice as long" (my paraphrase).

While the sentiment is right—we need more prayer for more strength for days when there is more to do—I bet Luther didn't have to get his kids to tap class.

But the more we are trying to accomplish, the more we need to rely on God. He is the architect of our day, as well as the one who provides the strength to make it through.

Do you not know?
  Have you not heard?
The LORD is the everlasting God,
  the Creator of the ends of the earth.
He will not grow tired or weary,
  and his understanding no one can fathom.
He gives strength to the weary
  and increases the power of the weak.
Even youths grow tired and weary,
  and young men stumble and fall;
but those who hope in the LORD
  will renew their strength.
They will soar on wings like eagles;
  they will run and not grow weary,
they will walk and not be faint.
        (Isaiah 40:28-31)

Zig Ziglar says it this way: "The story is told of a little guy valiantly but futilely trying to move a heavy log to clear a pathway to his favorite hideout. His dad stood nearby and finally asked him why he wasn't using all his strength. The little guy assured his dad he was straining with all his might. His dad quietly told him he was not using all his strength, because he hadn't asked him to help."

Is that how you are running through your day? Working and struggling, feeling as though you're expending all your energy but not making an inch's worth of progress? I describe those days as "swimming through molasses." When I get that feeling of going backward when all my energy is spent trying to move me forward, more often than not, those are the days that I have been "too busy to pray."

You are doing something pretty extraordinary over the next couple of weeks—taking some steps to start living out a God-given dream. So let's make sure the other areas of your life are in balance.

One of the beautiful things about having a specific goal is that it can give you great direction in other areas of your life. If you are goalless, it's easy to get off path. But a good solid goal out in front of you is like having a finish line at the end of a race. While you're focused on that finish line, there are only a few things you have to be concerned about (making sure you stay hydrated, making sure you're maintaining a doable pace) and a million things you don't have to worry about.

Prayer for Today

Father, I want to be focused on the areas that are important to You. Help me understand Your priorities for healthy living in every area of my life. Convict me in those areas that I need to rely more on You.

Getting Creative

Figure out creative ways to build quiet time into your day. Here are some ways that have worked for women I know:

- *Don't Leave Home Without It*—Keep a little journal (or your smartphone) with you to record all those things that you want to pray about. When you're waiting at a doctor's office or at the DMV, take a few moments to lift your requests to Him.

- *Dish Devotionals and Laundry Learnin'*—With so many kids in our house, a good chunk of my day is spent in front of my dishwasher and washing machine. Post verses that help you focus your mind on a certain subject. Do you need to work on patience? Post James 5:7-8. Trusting? Proverbs 3:5-6. Leave the verses up until they are memorized.

- *Learn on the Go*—I have memorized more Bible verses from kids' CDs than any Scripture memory program I have ever tried. Preview any CDs you buy to determine the "annoyance factor"—how many times you can listen to them before you fling them out of your car.

Project Reports

"Even though my goal is to take my jewelry design business to the next level, what has held me back in the past has nothing to do with business. I know that when I'm eating poorly, not sleeping, and not taking time with God, every other area of my life suffers. I get up 30 minutes earlier than I used to in order to get my day off to a better start. I spend 15 minutes in quiet time, and a few minutes doing something food-wise that is going to contribute to me eating well that week (putting my veggies in the slow cooker, mixing up a batch of low-fat brownies, making a shopping list). I have also decided to turn off my computer at 10:00 each night so I can let my brain start shutting down before I do."—Marie

Your Plan for the Project *(copy your plan on* The Me Project *Planner at the back of this book)*

Results

Project 9

Having a Mentor Moment
Finding a Mentor in Your Goal's Field

"Mentoring is a brain to pick, an ear to listen,
and a push in the right direction."
JOHN CROSBY

Your Project

Identify the style of mentoring that could work for you, and then make a list of a few people you would like to mentor you. (Bonus points if you actually ask them!)

Hi, Kathi...

We met last year in October when you spoke for the MOPS group at New Life Church in Alamo, CA. I'm the gal who put together the newsletter, introduced you at the meeting, and spoke with you about baby steps in pursuing speaking/writing "things."

(Are you getting a mental image yet?) You had mentioned something about putting together a newsletter and would I be interested in submitting articles, or perhaps editing. I said yes, but failed to follow through.

Career launch killed by time constraints. Story at 11...

So here it is, a year later and I'm still teetering on the edge of starting, but I think I'm getting ready to jump in...one toe at a time. Having said all that, I was wondering if we might chat sometime. I'd love to know if you're doing that newsletter we discussed and was wondering if we might find a way for me to work with you on that.

Before I ramble on, I'll wait to hear from you. It would be a blessing to connect, but I also see how busy your schedule is. Maybe we'll meet up, maybe not for a while.

Regardless, God's blessings to you.

Teresa Drake

I get e-mails like this about once a week. Someone has that burning desire to use the gifts and talents God has (or in a few cases, has not) given them for speaking or writing. It's usually from someone who has heard me speak or has read one of my books, and, as I did several years ago, recognized that's what she wants to do when she grows up.

I usually send a polite note and a list of resources to potential mentees. I have learned the hard way that every time I say yes to something valuable, I have to say no to something equally as valuable—such as sleep.

But this request was different. Teresa wasn't asking me to drop everything I was doing and spend some concentrated time developing her career. She was asking if she could contribute to what I already had going on in my ministry and learn from that.

Somebody wants to take part of my workload? How fast can they sign up?

Little did either of us know where that lunch meeting would lead us. Teresa has become my go-to girl for reading the first draft of my books, and she has worked on my newsletter and blog. In return, I've had the privilege of helping Teresa launch a speaking ministry and promoting her as a resource to moms' groups all over California. She is now speaking over 30 times a year to groups all over our area.

I would call that a win-win for both of us.

Some Benefits of Having a Mentor

Shorter Learning Curve

Your mentor has already done the research on things like:

- What materials are the best
- What books to read
- What groups to join
- What newsletter to subscribe to

Referrals and References

It's great to have an insider who can give you the tricks of the trade and tell you what training would be helpful, including what classes to take and which ones to avoid.

A Community of Like-Minded Devotees

When Marilyn Hilton, a wonderful nonfiction writer, agreed to have lunch with me, I was thrilled. We sat in a Tex-Mex restaurant, eating our weight in chips and salsa and talking about writers' conferences and book outlines. But the most valuable thing Marilyn did for me that day was let me in on a little secret: a group of Christian writers met once a month in a home in our area. Not only did she tell me that this clan existed, but she invited me to join them. I can point to that first meeting as a turning point in my career. Here I was, surrounded by women who not only loved writing, but were actually pursuing it as something more than a hobby. They talked about what was going on in the industry, who was buying books and who wasn't. What agents were a pleasure to work with, and those who were more of a nightmare. What conferences were well worth the money, and what books and blogs we absolutely must be reading.

Been There Done That Advice

Why spend all your time making the same mistakes and going down the same rabbit trails as other people in your chosen passion? Avoid duplicating the same mistakes that others have made by asking great questions: "Is there anything you wish you hadn't done in the first year of pursuing photography? A class that was a waste of time? Buying equipment that was overpriced and unnecessary?"

Worthy Feedback

I know your mom thinks you are the next Annie Leibovitz or Ansel Adams, but it might be better to listen to feedback from a person who is actually making a living taking pictures. A mentor can let you know whether there is something wrong that an untrained eye may miss.

How to Find a Mentor

Organically—Let God do the matchmaking

I met Debbie when I did a retreat for her church, which was located in my city. After she invited me to be part of a local group of women in ministry, I got to know her even better. Debbie has been a gift to me in so many ways. When I've received criticism, she's the one who can talk through it with me and put it in perspective. She really gets the ministry aspect of what I do and can help me figure out how to balance ministering to the women I love while still serving my family.

I need someone like Debbie to mentor me. She has a couple of years on me—her kids are planning weddings while mine are planning what college courses they're taking next semester—so the wisdom is there. She has keen insight into working in a male-dominated industry (the church) and how to play with the big boys (literally).

Stalking—Find someone who's doing what you want to do, and then hang out with her

When I first started speaking and writing, I met a woman who was several steps down the path from where I was. Jan Coleman was speaking at retreats and writing books, and she was kind enough to let me hang out at some of her events, go with her to a retreat she was speaking at, give me an outline to one of her book proposals that I could use as a guide, and generally just answer questions I had about how to do ministry.

Structured—through an organization or business

When my kids were little and I was a stay-at-home mom, one of my main sources of income was at-home parties. My manager, Patti Johnston, lived around the corner from me, and she taught me about running a business and devoting a portion of each day to working my work plan.

Internships

Several years ago, I had a little company where I would go into small businesses and just do whatever needed to be done. I loved being a support to women who were making their way in the world and watching them run their businesses up close and personal.

One of my favorite clients, Cynthia, was a well-respected wedding photographer. She was a one-woman show with me coming along sporadically to make appointments and run errands.

One of the ways that Cynthia would expand her workforce was to bring in interns. They would go to weddings with her and schlep her bags and carry her equipment. At the same time, they got a front row view of how to stage people for pictures, where to be during the wedding to get the best angles, and all that other insider information that a budding professional photographer needs.

When I first got started in speaking and writing, I would have done anything to just hang out with some of my favorite writers to see what goes on in "A Day in the Life of…" I knew I could learn so much from these women just by watching them in action. I remember saying about one of my favorite authors, "I would be happy to clean toilets if I could just hang out with her."

Now, if someone offers to let you clean toilets in order to hang out with her, it might be a good idea to check her motives (unless your dream is to own a housecleaning agency). However, if an opportunity arises to carry a photographer's camera bags to a wedding, to prep and chop for a cooking teacher, or to clean up for a favorite painting instructor, I would move a lot of things in my schedule to make that happen.

Most people who have had some success in their field are used to people asking to be mentored. But mentoring takes time—time that most busy people don't have to spare. But if you're willing to be at the bottom and help the expert get things done, you're going to learn more, and help more, than by buying them a cup of coffee.

Paid Mentoring

There's nothing wrong with having a mentor for hire. In fact, I think to consider paying for a mentor is a sign that you're moving down the road to your dreams.

I have hired professional mentors in a couple of different areas. Rob, my publicity guru, holds my feet to the fire and has high standards for every part of my ministry. I can attribute a lot of my growth to his time and effort. It seems expensive to put money into coaching, but I would rather spend a little money up front to get worthwhile advice than to waste time and money over a period of years going down the wrong path.

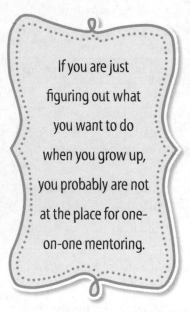

If you are just figuring out what you want to do when you grow up, you probably are not at the place for one-on-one mentoring.

Coaching is a huge industry, and a lot of people offer coaching services (at a significant cost). If you decide to go this route, make sure you have some great references from others before you plop down your hard-earned cash.

My other piece of advice is not to hire someone too quickly. If you are just figuring out what you want to do when you grow up, you probably are not at the place for one-on-one mentoring. Instead, read some books or take a class to figure out if you really enjoy stained-glass window making or if you just like the idea of stained-glass window making.

Few things can make a bigger difference in whether you succeed in your goal than having a mentor. That's why I want to give you a lot of ideas and avenues to pursue.

In the space below, start a list of the people you would love to have mentor you. Once you've thought of some, be creative in how that mentoring could work.

- Could you offer to do grunt work in her office for a couple of days—and get to see the inside operation?

- Could you tag along with an event planner to see how she preps a site?

- Could you be the assistant Bible study leader to learn more about teaching techniques from someone you admire?

- How about an online relationship? Could you offer to format a newsletter so you can see her process for putting it together?

Spend some time thinking creatively of what you might have to offer to the person you want to be mentored by—time, work, talent, money? Ask her if there's a way you could help.

And if you get rejected? That's why you have a list. Ask the next person. Ask God to bring the right people to mind, and just keep asking!

Prayer for Today

Father, I pray that I will be sensitive to who You put in my path. Let me learn to be a blessing to those I want to learn from.

Getting Creative

- In whatever area your passion lies, someone has been doing it (or some version of it) for a while. If it's someone you know, offer to buy them a cup of coffee and ask a lot of intelligent questions. I would never go into a meeting asking—or expecting—someone to mentor me. However, after a talk over a large cappuccino, you might get a better sense of where to get started and how to avoid some of the pitfalls your mentor has encountered in her journey.

Project Reports

"A mentor relationship is much like other relationships—not always easy to find a good one, one is not enough, and you never know where they'll lead you. I've been part of formal mentorship programs, but my best relationships are with people that I have come across naturally as opposed to the 'blind dates' formal programs set up. I've met them through being involved in things that interest me (schooling, organizations, volunteer activities, hobbies), and we've just clicked. I also have found that I look to different mentors for different things, just as I look to my spouse, girlfriends, family, and work colleagues for different types of support. My mentors are key to my path, and I'm sure these relationships will change and more will be developed as I travel down it."—Paige

"When I returned to school, I knew I wanted to major in arts administration, which is basically business administration with an emphasis on the arts and nonprofit organizations. The director of one of my favorite nonprofit arts organizations was my mentor for four years. I told her I was returning to school and asked if she'd be willing to act as a mentor, and she said yes."—Kristine

Your Plan for the Project *(copy your plan on* The Me Project *Planner at the back of this book)*

Results

Project 10

Asking for Directions
Keeping Our Goals in Front of God

"God does not give us everything we want, but He does fulfill His promises…leading us along the best and straightest paths to Himself."
DIETRICH BONHOEFFER

Your Project

Check in with God with some concentrated prayer and meditation (talking to and then listening to Him). Even if it's just for 10 minutes, get quiet with God and listen for His direction for your goal.

My husband and I had just landed at Tampa International Airport. While the purpose of our travel was to visit Roger's parents, we decided to sneak in some couple's time before heading to the family reunion. Roger had booked a romantic hotel on the beach only two miles from the airport.

Our combined food intake for the cross-country journey from California consisted of three bags of peanuts and half a box of Altoids I rescued from the bottom of my bag. We were anxious to stow our suitcases at the hotel and head out for our beachside dinner.

As we picked up our rental car, I was eager to try out the new navigational system Roger had just bought me. You see, I have a tendency to get lost while I'm driving, even in areas I've been to several times. Roger said he bought the new GPS for my safety. Really, I think he got tired of guiding me in like an air traffic controller every time I was more than three miles from the house.

I love my new mapping device—with one tiny exception. When I first turn on the display, Maggie (our pet name for our electronic guide) needs about 15 seconds to figure out where the satellite is. This process goes much faster if I stay put. If I start to drive, it could take up to two whole minutes for her to figure out where I am.

I have never been known as a patient woman. Even 15 seconds is about 14 seconds too long. Growing weary of waiting, I said to Roger, "Can't we just get going? It'll catch up with us." Roger knew the general direction of the hotel, so we hit the road. Our destination was only a couple of miles away. What could go wrong?

After a few minutes, and a turn onto an onramp, Maggie finally came blinking to life with directions and distance...22.2 miles! How did our "couple of miles away" hotel turn into a 22-mile trek?

That's when I discovered something called a causeway, which I'd never experienced in California. A causeway is a road that goes over a body of water. Like the body of water between the Tampa International Airport and St. Petersburg, Florida. Because there tends not to be a convenient place to turn around while traveling over water, and because our car was not Herbie the Love Bug with the ability to float, we were stuck going the whole distance over the causeway. And back— 22.2 miles round trip.

If only we had taken the 14 extra seconds to wait for directions instead of going off on our own, we would have saved time, aggravation, and grief.

Soon after our ill-fated trip, I was doing my morning devotions and this verse popped out at me:

> It is not good to have zeal without knowledge,
> nor to be hasty and miss the way.
> (Proverbs 19:2)

Who says God doesn't have a sense of humor?

Traveling with Maggie is a lot like figuring out the path God wants you to follow for your life and for your goals. The parallels show up for me almost every time I get lost. OK, almost every time I leave the house.

Gifts of the Maggie 1: You will be much better off if you wait for directions.

> Commit to the LORD whatever you do,
> and your plans will succeed.
> (Proverbs 16:3)

As women, we don't have an excess of time or energy to be heading off in the wrong direction while chasing after our dreams. We need a much simpler, direct route. Time and commitment spent up front praying and listening to God for direction will always be rewarded down the road.

Sometimes in my enthusiasm to get closer to my goals, I have an "Act Now, Pray Later" attitude. I get impatient and want to get going *now* with all the plans and dreams I have for my life. When I act out of desire, enthusiasm, or trying to simply check things off my list, I usually end up wasting time, energy, and emotion.

> God has a lot of rewards for those who wait on direction from Him.

Like Maggie, God has a lot of rewards for those who wait on direction from Him. When I pray before I act, I may not have clear direction all at once. What I can be sure of is that I have put my plans before God. I am honoring Him first in everything I do, every plan I make.

Gifts of the Maggie 2: You don't need to know every turn that's coming up—you just need to know what your next step is.

> "Therefore do not worry about tomorrow, for tomorrow will worry about itself. Each day has enough trouble of its own" (Matthew 6:34).

Don't ever try to give me directions over the phone. I'm good for about two turns, and then my brain starts to think about the Discovery Channel special I saw last night, or tries to figure out when the cute pink bag I saw at the mall might go on sale. When I get directions all at once, trying to hold everything in my head about the next eight turns I need to make, it is almost always a guarantee I'm going to get hopelessly lost, confused, frustrated, and off track. The beauty of Maggie is that she gives you only the next turn you have to make.

As busy women, we can get bogged down by the magnitude of all we have to do. If we start to look too closely at all that's involved in having a rewarding career or raising great kids and pursuing our dream, it would be very easy to get completely overwhelmed.

A better approach is to take each day as it comes. Planning for the future is great. Worrying about it will get you nowhere. Keep your final destination in mind and concern yourself with the turn just ahead of you. God is the only one who can see around the corner.

The other benefit of just focusing on the turn right in front of you and not worrying about the next seven is that you get to enjoy the ride. When you have a dream that is bigger than yourself, there are many opportunities to step out in faith and see God's hand working in your life.

I tend to miss the miracles in the moment when I'm worrying about what has to happen next month. Just concentrate on the next turn and enjoy the ride.

Gifts of the Maggie 3: Trust the directions, even if they are different from what you expect.

> Whether you turn to the right or to the left, your ears will hear a voice behind you, saying, "This is the way; walk in it" (Isaiah 30:21).

Sometimes for fun I will check out Maggie's directions to a familiar place, just to see if she has a different way of getting there. Often she will direct me to a shortcut I didn't know about or a new road I had yet to discover. I've learned a lot by taking routes different from my normal routines.

Today, I want you to spend some time just checking in with God. *Am I going in the right direction? Do You want me to press forward on something or wait?* Learning to be sensitive to God's leading is a skill we can develop.

Prayer for Today

God, I want to be sensitive to your leading. Give me ears to hear your voice and eyes to see your path.

Getting Creative

- Make a date with yourself to go to your favorite coffee bar and sit and pray.

- Have small kids at home? Whenever my friend Kim needed some quiet time, she would put herself in the kids' playpen. It really did give her a few minutes to herself.

- Sit in your car to pray during your lunch break at work.

- Some of my best praying gets done on my walks with my dog. I have to unplug from my iPod, but it is always so worth it.

Project Reports

"When I first decided to go back to school, my husband and I felt like this was God's leading, but we weren't sure how to pay for it. Every step in the process went smoothly, though, so Rob said, 'Just keep stepping forward,' and that's what I did. I figured the meeting with the financial aid counselor would be the end of the line, but instead a smiling face tapped a few keys on her computer, initialed a couple of forms, and I was on my way. I couldn't believe it!

"When I'm having a rough time keeping up with the workload, or feeling guilty about not having a full-time job, somebody will say exactly what I needed to hear to know that God is still there and I'm still on track. I especially love those moments when God's answer to the cry of your heart rings out at a time and place that you least expected, and suddenly everything is all right again."—Melissa

"I was very young when God called me to be a speaker. I know He called me to do it, even though my children were still little at the time. The very same year He called me to be a speaker, He also called me to put my children in a University Model School, which allows students to attend classes two days a week and me to homeschool them three days a week. I felt as if God had given me the best of both worlds, and I was excited about what He had planned for my future.

"It wasn't long, however, until people started cautioning me about being a speaker while my children were so young. Since I knew several of these people had my best interests at heart, I prayed some more about it. Was I doing this because I wanted to be a speaker or was this really what God had for me? Were these people correct that I should wait until my children were older? I prayed and prayed for wisdom, because I knew that I had only a few precious years with my children and did not want to miss out on any time with them.

"Time and time again, though, God helped me realize it was He who was calling me to be a speaker. He said I was exactly where He wanted me. He reassured me that the reason I was called to have my girls at a UMS school was so that I would not lose that time with them. Although the words that people said to me hurt at first, I realized I needed to be thankful for them because they caused me to seek God's face for His reassurance that I am exactly where He wants me to be."—Andrea

Your Plan for the Project *(copy your plan on* The Me Project *Planner at the back of this book)*

Results

Investing in Your Passion
Setting Aside the Time, Money, Energy, and Space to Make Your Goals a Reality

"Get over the idea that only children should spend their time in study. Be a student so long as you still have something to learn, and this will mean all your life."

Henry L. Doherty

Your Project

Find the classes, seminars, and workshops you should be taking, and then make a plan to take them.

Never in the history of the world has there been a time such as this where it is so easy to be a student. You can research online, go to Wikipedia (and double check with other sources), you can be part of a teleconference, a webinar, go to a community college, get a coach, go to a conference, or get podcasts uploaded to your iPod.

Have you taken a class or some sort of training in the area of your passion? If not, why not?

Excuses for Not Learning

"I don't have the time."

I understand life is busy, but there is no excuse for not learning. If you really have no time (you're a single mom with no back up; you're working full-time with small kids), you can still listen to seminars on CD or podcasts from the Internet. I listen to sermons on my iPod while doing the laundry and cleaning the kitchen. Sometimes I listen for spiritual teaching, and sometimes I'm checking out a speaker's teaching technique. I listen to podcasts while driving to and from jobs, and I listen to Audible.com books while I'm walking our dog.

Let me challenge you on something. Do you value teaching and education only for your kids? Wouldn't you hate it if your kids stopped learning when they had kids? I want you to keep learning about and leaning into your passion every single day. I want you to learn enough about your goal to see if it's really worth pursuing.

Keep learning about and leaning into your passion every single day.

"I don't know where to find a class."

This excuse always cracks me up. I don't care what your goal is or where your passion lies, there is someone somewhere teaching a class on it.

When I was starting my own business, I went to local seminars on how to do just that. They were offered by the Chamber of Commerce and were incredibly informative. Our local library offers a ton of classes in every area you can think of—from publishing a book to learning a language. Check out these sources:

- Local universities or community colleges

- Google (just type in your passion + classes and see what pops up)

- Adult education through online distance learning or your parks and recreation department

- Stores—many grocery stores now offer cooking classes, or check out your local craft store if beading is your new passion

"It would be too expensive."

Maybe you're right—but do you know exactly how much it's going to cost? The money you spend on a class could help you avoid time and money wasters down the road. So figure out how much that class is and then see if there might be cheaper options. And if your budget is really tight, consider setting aside a little each month in a training fund you can tap into later.

Prayer for Today

I know that curiosity comes from You. I pray that I will never stop learning the things that You want me to know.

Getting Creative

Some places to check out for classes on specific topics:

- Cooking—Whole Foods, wineries, culinary schools (many have seminars for nonprofessionals)

- Cake decoration—community college, bakeries, cake supply stores

- Photography—community college, photo supply stores, photography clubs

- Interior design—home furnishing stores, Home Depot, paint stores

Project Reports

"A girlfriend and I had heard about some chocolate truffle-making classes, and we decided to take a class together for fun. Chocolate classes? What could be more fun than that, right? We learned truffles and all kinds of other candies. It was so exciting knowing that with this knowledge we could make fantastic gifts for people and look like a professional. Imagine the money we would save! This idea, after many weeks of no sleep from excitement, developed into a fast-growing and fun business that involves my whole family. I am so glad I went to that little class!"—Cheryl

"I am culinarily challenged. Or at least I was when I got married. It felt like an overwhelming task to research a recipe, shop for the myriad ingredients, pull off a meal after work, and then find—I had to do it again tomorrow! We could eat only so much roast chicken breast. I watched the ease and creativity of the Food Network stars with envy. I thought some people just had the knack, and that we were destined for an unhealthy stream of take-out cuisine.

"So when the local Whole Foods Cooking School advertised for volunteers to help prep ingredients for cooking classes, I was intrigued, especially by the phrase 'no experience necessary.' What a great way to gain firsthand experience with unheard of ingredients on someone else's dime. I wasn't about to risk $25 a pound on fish that I would likely ruin. But I'd welcome an expert chef walking me through the preparation process. And I was willing to chop (lots of chopping) and scrub (lots of pots and pans).

"Two years and many hours of chopping and scrubbing later, I feel confident that I can cook a whole chicken, make a great sauce, or add more than tomatoes and ranch on a salad. Having others over is a fun challenge rather than drudgery. On the path to discover a way to get through one of life's daily routines more efficiently, I found a new hobby that engages my creativity and thrills my husband's taste buds!"—Ashley

Your Plan for the Project *(copy your plan on* The Me Project *Planner at the back of this book)*

Results

Project 12

Peer Pressure for Grown-Ups
Getting a Couple of People to Hold You Accountable

"Pressure makes diamonds."

GENERAL GEORGE S. PATTON

Your Project

Find a couple of women to hold you accountable for your goal.
It could be the women you are already working through this
book with, or it could be women who have the same goals as
you do.

Every woman has done it. You get up early New Year's morning.
You write down your goals on a piece of paper. If you are really bold,
you post them on the fridge for the rest of your family to see. And that's
where it ends. You have no one checking in with you, no one holding you accountable. Your husband certainly is not going to ask you,
"Hey, it says here on your New Year's resolutions that you're going to
the gym five times a week. How's it going?" No, he is not going to ask.
He is smarter than that.

This is the point where a woman needs a couple of good, godly
women in her life. Women who are assigned to ask the Project Manager (you) the tough questions and keep her going down the road God
has set out for her.

You Goal Girl!

The waitress knows that we are in deep discussion so, instead of
refilling our ceramic mugs, this time she just leaves the pot of coffee.

She is used to this scene—the three of us friends talking, laughing until we have to "Shush!" each other, as well as stopping to pray along the way. We are the Goal Girls, and this table is our monthly meeting spot.

The Goal Girls started several years ago when every area of my life was in transition. My marriage was falling apart, and I found myself back in the job market to support myself and my kids. On top of all that, I needed to find a new place to live. I felt as though everything was spinning out of control.

I knew that I also needed to make some changes in other areas of my life. Spending time with God had become a faint memory for me. I wanted to reconnect, but I was having trouble being committed to my day-to-day relationship with Him.

I needed support that was more than a once-a-week Bible study. I needed people around me to love and guide me through this hurtful time in my life.

At the same time, my friend Vikki, a 30-year-old wife and mother, was just plain overwhelmed. With her two active kids and another on the way, she was feeling the pressures of keeping it all together. In addition to taking care of her family, Vikki worked outside the home several nights a month, and she was the women's ministry leader at our growing church. The fast pace of Vikki's life was threatening to swallow her up if she didn't makes some changes immediately.

Another friend, Angela, young and vibrant at 34, had an even more desperate situation. Her health was in serious jeopardy, which complicated her busy life caring for her two small girls, and she knew she had to take some radical steps, including exercising and losing weight, to start restoring herself physically.

All of us were longing for change. We wanted to live healthier lives, not just physically, but also emotionally and spiritually. Each of us needed help figuring out what God designed us to do, but we also needed to make sure that we stayed on track—someone to hold our feet to the fire.

I asked Angela and Vikki if they would be interested in forming an accountability group. I was honest and upfront: "I have no idea how it will work, but I am so frustrated and scared that I'm willing to try just about anything. I guess we can just make it up as we go along?" Apparently, they were just as desperate, and we decided to meet the following week.

That was eight years ago, and we are still supporting each other, praying for each other, and holding each other in godly accountability.

Starting an Accountability Group

What Is Accountability?

Accountability is simply having to report to someone the progress you are making on an activity. When you work in an office, you're accountable to a boss for the work she assigns you. Even if you are a self-starter, most of us need that little bit of outside pressure to get our jobs done well and on time. What do you do when you're running a household, your own business, and your own life, and there is no boss to answer to? Asking other women to hold you accountable is a great way to have a little bit of that outside pressure to help you stay on track.

Vikki, Angela, and I sacrifice time from our overcrowded lives to stay accountable to one another because it's biblical and it works. Proverbs 27:17 (NLT) says, "As iron sharpens iron, so a friend sharpens a friend." Being with one another and holding one another accountable keeps us focused and on task.

How Is an Accountability Group Different Than a Support Group?

Generally support groups focus either on a stage of life (including moms' groups or after divorce groups) or a specific area to overcome (Overeaters Anonymous or Alcoholics Anonymous). These groups can have dozens of members at each meeting. While support groups offer an environment to meet with others who are in your situation and the opportunity to learn and be encouraged, there is generally a lower level of follow-up for individual members.

Accountability groups offer the chance to meet with one or two other people in order to stay focused on whatever area of your life you are trying to grow in at that time. While neither Angela nor Vikki are writers or stepmothers, they are able to hold me accountable in those areas by following up on the goals I've set for myself and shared with them at past gatherings.

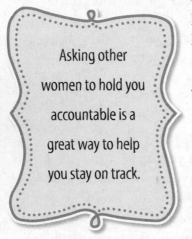

Asking other women to hold you accountable is a great way to help you stay on track.

What Accountability Looks Like for Us

We come to our once-a-month meetings with our goals already written out. I dedicate one sheet of paper to each area of my life. There is a page dedicated to health, another for important relationships in my life, one for household management, and so on. Sometimes my goal list will be much longer in one area than another. When one of my kids needs special attention, or I have a good friend who is going through a tough time, I may have several goals on my "Relational" page, but almost none in another area.

Along with each goal, we set a target date that we want to see the goal completed by. For instance, on my "Spiritual" goal sheet, I might write:

Goal	Date of Completion
Join Bible study	September 15

When we write out our goals, we try to be specific and realistic. Instead of setting a goal to become a better cook, I might write, "Try three new main courses from the Greek cookbook," or "Sign up for the Asian cooking class at the community center."

When I started to focus more on spending time with God, Angela reminded me to be specific and realistic. At first, I had written, "Spend forty-five minutes every day in prayer and quiet time." Angela graciously said, "Kath, how are you going to go from zero to forty-five minutes? Why don't you start with five minutes a day and build on that." From that five-minute block of time, I have grown into having a meaningful and significant quiet time every day.

When we first started meeting eight years ago, we were in for a reality check. Over the first few months, we learned to gently say to each other, "Wow, that looks like a lot to accomplish with two kids and everything else going on in your life. Is it realistic? Is there something that you could give up or move to another month?" We have learned to protect each other from overextending ourselves, and in turn, have learned to take care of our own schedules and bodies.

The next time we get together, we give each person forty minutes to go over the previous month's goals and set out her vision for the next month. We make copies of our goals that we can pass out to the other two. That way, we have an easier time checking in with each other.

Between each meeting, we stay up-to-date on where each of us is in meeting our goals, as well as asking for additional support when we need it. For example, the weeks before I moved to a different city, I needed more support to stay focused and on track with getting my house packed up and ready to be sold. During those pressure-filled weeks, I would receive several phone calls a day asking how my plan was going. Just knowing that Vikki or Angela could be calling at any moment gave me the extra push I needed to stay on track and tackle what had to be done.

You can also have an accountability group focused on one specific area of your life. I have separate groups for more complex goals I'm currently working on for my health and writing. These groups give me the special support I need to accomplish bigger projects in those areas.

The Benefits of Accountability

Our group has gotten the three of us through life together. Angela and Vikki have prayed and held me accountable through the hardest time of my life. During the rough days, it was a huge comfort to know that I had two godly women who knew what I was going through and could remind me that God had designed me for a greater purpose than what I felt like at the moment.

Following my divorce, I wrestled with where God was in my life. I felt abandoned and unloved. Vikki and Angela reminded me of all that God had brought me through and pointed out all the ways that God continued to care for me even when I couldn't feel His presence.

Getting through rough times is a blessing, but the most thrilling part of accountability is seeing the progress in each other's lives. It's been an honor to stand with Angela and Vikki as I've seen them accomplish goals that none of us would have dreamed possible just a few short years ago. From keeping our houses clean, to losing weight, to opening a small business, to walking a half marathon—no goal is too big to not be supported. On the flip side, no goal is too small that it's not celebrated when it's reached.

The biggest honor was to have these two ladies who had walked me back to a place of loving and growing in God, a place of health and healing, celebrate with me as bridesmaids at my wedding to Roger. These women were celebrating not only the future I had with Roger, but the past that they had walked me through to get to the place where I could be part of a healthy marriage.

Dare to Dream

After hearing how Goal Girls has impacted our lives, several other women have followed our model. Are there some women in your life who you would love to have hold you accountable and do life with? Ask them. When you are committed to living the life God has planned for you, He will provide a path to get there. He also is faithful to provide others to walk that path with you. Take advantage of the women God has sent into your life to make your God-given dreams a reality.

Prayer for Today

Heavenly Father, I pray that You would bring into my life women I can build up and who can hold me up as I reach for my goal.

Getting Creative

- If you are trying to work toward a goal and are just never able to fit in the small steps that you need to accomplish, maybe it's time to apply some healthy peer pressure to your project. If your goal is to run a marathon, how about signing up with a friend to go to Weight Watchers or making an appointment to train together?

- See if other women in your MOPS or Bible study group are working toward similar goals as you. There is just something about the buddy system—people who are invested in your success and are willing to call you when you don't show up.

Project Reports

"Putting things in writing and setting goals is huge. Sometimes we keep our dreams secret and this doesn't help at all. Other things that have helped me:

- Sharing my goal(s) in small group and asking them to pray for me (and then they love it and rejoice with me when I succeed)

- Forming a prayer team for a big hairy audacious goal (like writing a book)

- Breaking down a specific goal into steps and charting progress on my whiteboard. I keep this right by my desk. What an amazing visual reminder.

- Meeting and talking to other people who are a little further down the road to success. Their skills and strengths rub off on me.

- Setting incremental goals and having a friend keep me accountable."—Susy

"I did a triathlon and joined Team In Training, and that helped me have people who held me accountable as well as trained me for the event…all the while getting in shape and raising money for a great cause!"—Vashie

You may want to partner with someone with the same goal. Look how my friend Dineen Miller describes her writing partnership with coauthor Lynn Donovan:

"After writing fiction on my own for so long, writing nonfiction with a partner was an interesting change. The key factor that worked for us was that our focus always remained on the purpose of our ministry. The division of chapters and portions of our book came easily when we each brought our strengths to the table and were honest about our weaknesses. We both knew we could not write this book alone.

"We shuttled our pieces back and forth for input, spent hours on the phone brainstorming sections, and worked in tandem on joint areas like the introduction and leader's guide. Having that kind of input from each other just made the book even stronger.

"My background in graphic design taught me that the best ideas come from multiple minds sharing and adding. I find this to be true of writing as well."

Your Plan for the Project *(copy your plan on* The Me Project *Planner at the back of this book)*

Results

Dancing Cows:
The Chick-fil-A Way to Rest
Resting Your Way to Success

"The hurrier I go, the behinder I get."

BUMPER STICKER ON A SPEEDING CAR

Your Project

Schedule times of real rest in your day, week, and month as you work toward your goals.

I sigh as Roger and I take Highway 17 toward Santa Cruz, driving over the mountains toward the beach and the boardwalk, surrounded by redwoods and local farms and state parks.

"Do you realize how blessed we are to live where we do?" I said.

"Yes," Roger replied. "And if I didn't, you saying it every day of our marriage would remind me."

I didn't realize how deep my love for the Bay Area ran until Roger pointed out the frequency of my comments about it. (He should be doubly grateful—I was born in Northern California; he moved here from Indiana where digging his car out of the snow was a common occurrence.)

But can you blame me? We live less than half a day's drive from almost anything you can think of: the beach during the summer, the mountains during ski season, San Francisco when a musical is coming through, great ethnic restaurants, and not once have I had to dig my car out of a snow bank.

There's only one thing missing from our little corner of paradise—a Chick-fil-A.

If you have not experienced the perfection that is the Chick-fil-A chicken sandwich, let me describe it for you. It's a chicken patty breaded and deep fried in peanut oil (trust me, it works), then served on a buttered bun with two pickle slices. (They say you can add tomatoes and lettuce, but why ruin it with healthy stuff?)

Chick-fil-A also has a healthy menu. Whatever.

I love Chick-fil-A and what they stand for and their chicken sandwiches so much that at one point, I had a Google alert for articles about how they run their business. (I'm not just a fan, I'm a super fan.) As I started to read more about their values and how they run their business, I fell in love with them for more than their deep-fried chicken breast.

This is an amazing company that values their employees and customers. Chick-fil-A is very selective about who gets to sling that chicken. "It's easier to get a job in the CIA than to own a Chick-fil-A franchise" is a favorite saying at the corporate office. They have one of the highest employee retention rates in any service industry. Part of that is the careful screening they do before hiring someone. Another reason? No Chick-fil-A restaurant is open on Sunday.

While visiting our friends Steve and Shannon in Colorado Springs, they introduced us to Chick-fil-A and then told us the closed-on-Sunday policy. I know that Steve and Shannon are intelligent people, but I honestly believed they had to be mistaken. Fast-food restaurants are not closed for a whole day. I had worked in the service industry enough to know that Sunday was a major money-making day.

Industry experts were baffled as well. But listen to this response that Dan Cathy, president and chief operating officer of Chick-fil-A, gave to talk-show host Dave Ramsey when Dave asked about the business sense of closing on Sundays.

> Our corporate purpose is to glorify God by being the faithful steward of all He has entrusted to us and have a positive influence on people. But as a businessperson it really does work for us. It makes a difference. We are more rested on Monday because we've been able to take the day off to rest and renew

ourselves. Our smiles are bigger, and I think even our drive-thrus run a little faster on Monday because we had Sunday off.

We are not built 24/7. God built our body to have eight hours of sleep and to take some time off. And we found that we pick up on that productivity. Any business we lose on Sunday we more than make up for with better service and a better atmosphere on Monday.

Sabbath—Not Just for Old Testament Folks

OK, there's some stuff in the Bible that doesn't make a whole bunch of sense to me:

> "Do not mate different kinds of animals.
> "Do not plant your field with two kinds of seed.
> "Do not wear clothing woven of two kinds of material."
>   (Leviticus 19:19)

And I have to admit, observing the Sabbath was one of those rules that felt a lot like the instructions not to mix a cotton-weave with a poly-blend. A bit antiquated.

Observing a Sunday off is a hard thing. My agent, Rachelle, said, "If I want to observe a Sabbath, I need to prepare for six hours on Saturday to be able to rest on Sunday. If my husband wants to observe a Sabbath, he takes a nap."

But the more that Roger and I are intentional about having a day to rest, a day to put away our computers, not work, and focus on God, our family, and restoring ourselves physically, emotionally, and spiritually, the more we feel able to slide back into work having taken our stress down a level or two.

I have discovered that when I indulge

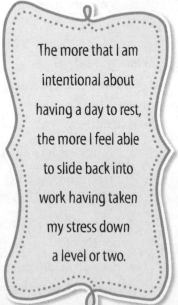

The more that I am intentional about having a day to rest, the more I feel able to slide back into work having taken my stress down a level or two.

in the false economy of trying to get more done by working seven days a week, not only do I suffer, but my goals suffer. That's why I want you to rest your way to success.

- Make sure you have some down time every week where your focus is not on getting things done but on getting deeper with God and with community and on getting rest.

- Make sure you have a beginning and an end to each week.

- Make sure you have a beginning and an end to each work day. No spreading work from eight in the morning until ten at night.

I know the last thing you would expect is for me to say, "Work less." But I want you to make sure that you don't burn out. I want you to be living a life that is full of God-adventure for years to come.

So in the space below "Your Plan for the Project," write when you are going to rest.

Prayer for Today

Help me not to feel guilty when I rest, but to be able to completely rest in You.

Getting Creative

Whether your Sabbath is on Sunday or, because of work schedules, you have picked another day of the week, here are some things you can do in advance to make that one day as restful as possible:

- Freeze meals in advance that you can just stick in the oven.

- Prep some ingredients for your slow cooker the day before, and then dump them in before you leave for church.

- Let your kids in on the plan to rest—no trips to the mall; no rides to a friend's house.

- Save up some activities: a movie to watch or a book to read. Make a date with yourself.

Project Reports

"Something I still struggle with is taking a day to rest. I am a workhorse and have two jobs: a main one and a fun one that is very part-time. I keep them both because I love them both. I am married, I teach Sunday school, work with the youth group, I am part of a few committees at church—the list goes on. I often feel that I need to take time to slow down and rest and spend more time with God. I've had to learn the hard way that it's better to spend time with Him than to run around trying to do things for Him."—Jessica

"My Bible study group just did a lesson on taking a 'really and for-true' (to quote my kids) Sabbath. My family and I attend church services in the morning. Then we head home, change into our comfy clothes, and just kick back. We read, we talk together, we watch a movie together, and most times we nap. Meals are courtesy of the leftovers in the fridge. No prep, just get what you want. The main focus is little to *no* work at all this day and to spend a restful time with family."—Cheryl

Your Plan for the Project *(copy your plan on* The Me Project *Planner at the back of this book)*

Results

Project 14

Set Yourself Up for Success
Making an Appointment with Yourself

"You will never find time for anything. You must make it."
CHARLES BUXTON

Your Project

Put an appointment into your week that will force you closer
to your goal, whether it's an appointment with yourself, with
a group of like-minded people, or with a partner.

"Sixteen-ounce drip with sugar-free vanilla and a bran muffin?" It's
posed as a question, but it's anything but. The barista doesn't even look
up to confirm that is indeed my order. She knows, because it has been
my order the other 200 times I've gone into Orchard Valley Coffee.

Every Monday and Thursday for the past year and a half, I have
gone to the writer-friendly coffee house to meet up with other people
who are working on their books. Cathy is working on her second
novel—this one is women's fiction. Shelley has written over a dozen
books, and her current passion is young adult fiction. Katie writes
intense, action-packed adventure novels. Someone is always running
from the police or fashioning some sort of weapon.

As much as I love the idea of sitting at my computer with my dog at
my feet and a steaming cup of coffee next to me, working on the next
chapter of my book, it's almost impossible for me to write at home. As
soon as I sit at my desk, the previously silent washer and dryer beckon
me to start just one load. Once that load is started, I notice that the
trash bag in the laundry area desperately needs to be emptied. As long

It's not always a straight upward climb to getting our goals accomplished.

as I'm taking out the trash, I might as well get all the trash from upstairs too. Is it any wonder that I have trouble finishing a chapter at home?

But at the coffee shop, I get things done. Yes, when we get together we sometimes talk too much—we catch up on each other's writing, what we're reading, and what's going on in the writing world. But when it comes to actually writing, I get a ton more done in the company of fellow writers than I do in the company of my dog.

Here are just some of the benefits I have experienced by getting together twice a week with fellow writers:

Accountability

I talk big at the beginning of the month about how many words I will write, the articles I will research, and the chapters I will get done. At the coffee house, however, I'm held accountable for my big talk. Sometimes we have very loose accountability. (Hey, have you finished those 5000 words you were going to get done this week?) Other times, it's a little more serious. I had a pretty firm deadline this month and needed some this-will-be-painful-if-I-don't-accomplish-it accountability. So this month, if I didn't write 10,000 words, I had to give three of my coffeehouse friends foot rubs. To say that I was motivated to finish is a bit of an understatement.

Encouragement

It's not always a straight upward climb to getting our goals accomplished. There are plenty of people out there telling me no to things I want to do. It is great to have some friends who can see the whole picture while I focus on the no.

Fun

I look forward to getting together with these women. This is my tribe who not only have my back, but can discuss in detail last night's episode of *Glee*.

Prayer

I need people who have my back—and since these ladies are there for the week-to-week drama of my life, they stay on top of when I need prayer backup and actually follow up to find out how it's going.

Prayer for Today

Thank You for the gift of other people who hold my feet to the fire.

Getting Creative

- Can't find someone who is pressing toward the same goal? Then recruit a friend or two so you can hold each other accountable for your individual goals.

- Cold call local groups and see what is a good fit. Just because a group is close to your house doesn't make it the right group for you.

Project Reports

"This year, to get more in touch with my creative side, I have jumped into taking classes. I've taken some watercolor classes from a local artist and a graphic design class at the community college. I joined the local art association and just recently joined the graphics team at church. I'm also entering my work in shows when I can. I want to be around people in the field. It's inspiring to see what others are working on, and I think it pushes my creativity to try things I never would have thought of. I think it makes my work way better.

"I'm also doing an online forensic art class, which is the overall goal I'm trying to pursue. It's taking me forever to finish. All these things are moving me closer to the goal. My husband is also very creative in audio production, so he totally supports me in the creative process, and I him. I think his support helps me believe more in what I'm doing and helps me keep going."—Sandra

Your Plan for the Project *(copy your plan on* The Me Project *Planner at the back of this book)*

Results

Week Three Projects

I Said Board, Not Bored
Creating Your Own Board of Directors

"As iron sharpens iron, so a friend sharpens a friend."
PROVERBS 27:17 NLT

Your Project

Create your own board of directors. This will help you toward this goal—and possibly other areas of your life.

Let's be honest, following your God-given dreams can be lonely. When I'm trying to make decisions about my goals and my ministry, I need some smart and strategic people to bounce ideas off of. This is why I wanted—no, *needed*—to create my own board of directors.

All the successful women I know have surrounded themselves with other women who will encourage, mentor, and, with love and firmness, even correct them in life and in ministry. In my life, these people are my board.

My board of directors (BOD) is a group of people who are experts on me. Besides my husband, my BOD consists of five friends who know me well and are willing to invest the time and energy to help me achieve my goals.

A board of directors is different from your accountability partners. Your BOD helps you create the vision and the steps for your goal; your accountability partners help you make it happen, day to day.

My BOD runs like a real board of directors too. We meet once or twice a year to go over the direction of my life and my ministry, and then we brainstorm how to make my ministry goals happen.

When a major decision needs to be made—What is the focus of my next book? Am I maintaining something close to balance in my ministry and personal life?—these people can give me wise input. They know my weaknesses and my strengths. They know my temperament and the right questions to ask before I make a major change.

Need some godly wisdom in your life? Who could you bring on "board"?

When you're working toward your goal, it helps to have input from people who are not directly involved with making your goal happen. They can look at things from a different angle, as well as see some opportunities for growth and development you may have missed.

Types of Women to Consider for Your Board

So, who should you ask to be on your board? Here are just a few types of women you may want to consider:

The Connection Queen

This is the person who knows *everybody*. From the school principal to the owner of the Pilates studio, she knows everyone and what is going on in their lives.

Marci is the sales director at a local retreat center, and she knows everyone. Not only has she connected me with some great women's ministry leaders and worship leaders, she put me in contact with Monica, who became my assistant.

The Wise Sage

She is the person who has been there, done that, and learned from the experience. She can give you words of advice and perspective when things seem out of control. Are things not going according to plan? Kids behaving badly? Oh honey, has she got some stories for you. She is also the first person to suggest that perhaps you (a creative type) should hire an accountant if you want to stay out of jail.

My sage is Carol. She has been a women's ministry leader for more years than I have been a grown-up woman. She is great because she understands my audience—not just the women sitting at the conferences I teach at, but also the women planning the events.

The Brainy Cheerleader

You need people cheering you on—people who believe in the possibility of you. You also want people who know your strengths and weaknesses.

Angela and I have been good friends for years, and she is one of my biggest supporters.

The Planner

This person asks the tough questions. She will most likely be one of those friends who plans everything in advance—annoying, but necessary.

For me this is Terri. She's part of a family-run business and knows to look at things from every angle. She asks the tough questions, but supports me 100 percent.

In the Industry

This person is already a player in the area you are working toward. She knows the people, the places to go, the classes to take, and the e-mail loops to be on.

Author and speaker Susy Flory is my industry go-to girl. She has published several books and knows the ins and the outs of the industry.

The Spiritual Character of Your Board

You may already have some people in mind for your board of directors. Great! Make sure they have not only the talents to be on your board, but also the spiritual depth and character to contribute in a healthy way.

Here are some of the character qualities to look for as you assemble your board of directors:

1. They put God first in their life.

If your goal is to follow God's plan for your life, you'll want to

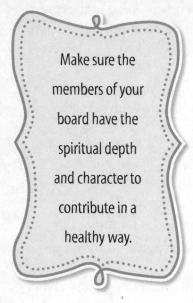

Make sure the members of your board have the spiritual depth and character to contribute in a healthy way.

surround yourself with other people who have gone down that same road.

2. They are successful in their field.

Your board members may have run their own Fortune 500 company or they may be the biggest prayer warriors you know. Whatever their area of expertise, they know what it takes to be successful and have put in the hard work to make it happen.

3. They are interested in seeing you succeed.

Since a board of directors has a vested interest in seeing the company they provide oversight for succeed (whether they are stockholders or simply believe in the cause), you want to invite on your board people who are in your corner and want to see you live out your dreams.

How It Works

It may not look as formal as the meetings of my board of directors (meeting in person in a hotel conference room with someone taking minutes), but you could have a once-a-quarter chat via Skype, or pick two people who are great brainstormers and take them out for coffee (your treat, of course).

As with every other relationship you have, make sure this is a win-win situation for your board. Be willing to invest in their lives and dreams as they have in yours.

Decide when you will meet and how often. You could do this short-term for a smaller goal or long-term if it's a life-changing goal. For my ministry, I meet with my board once or twice a year, but we keep in contact by e-mail and phone throughout the year. If I have a smaller, specific goal—working on a book, for instance—I will select a smaller group for input for that project, and we will meet every few weeks for a shorter period of time (maybe a few months). I suggest you come with an agenda of what you want to talk about and, for a more formal board of directors, send it to everyone beforehand. That will give people the opportunity to think and pray about what you plan to discuss.

Listen to your board of directors. Don't waste board members' time if you already know what you're going to do and just want someone to rubber stamp it for you. That doesn't mean you need to do everything your board says—when it comes down to it, my husband and I are the final decision-makers—but we always listen carefully to my board's advice.

Find those friends who can help you stay true to the calling God has put in your life. Trust me, they will be glad (and honored) that you asked.

Prayer for Today

God, help me to seek wise counsel in everything I do.

Getting Creative

- You may have your board already formed. It may consist of a couple of moms from your PTA group that you meet up with for coffee, or maybe your husband and sister are the perfect people to give you advice and brainstorm with you. It doesn't have to be formal or elaborate.

- If several of your friends are working on the same goal, you may want to establish yourselves as a board that serves each other.

Project Reports

"I meet once a month with a group called Circle of Influence (by invitation, sponsored by a well-known Christian author). We discuss writing, speaking, and marketing. This author has poured into my life for more than two years, and I've grown

tremendously in the areas of confidence, publishing knowledge, and practical skills. We have built-in accountability."
—Dawn

Your Plan for the Project *(copy your plan on* The Me Project *Planner at the back of this book)*

Results

Working on Your Goals When You Don't Have Time to Work on Your Goals

Finding Time to Make It All Happen

"Yesterday is a canceled check; tomorrow is a promissory note;
today is the only cash you have—so spend it wisely."

KAY LYONS

Your Project

Identify the little spots of time you have right now to make progress on your goals.

How to Waste Time on Your Laptop: An Expert's Guide
(or My Real-Life Strategy for Getting Things Done)

Don't you just love your computer! It's such a timesaving device. I can do my banking, order groceries, talk to my agent, invite friends over via evite.com, and design my next newsletter anywhere in the world that has a Verizon tower nearby. It's amazing all the tasks I can complete with the aid of a power outlet.

So why have I spent a large part of my summer playing Free Cell?

I have just hit some major deadlines in my life after 18 months of running full steam ahead. I realized just this last week I am apparently not capable of work unless I am under tremendous pressure and have a sense of overwhelming guilt. I just kind of sit there thinking, "I know I have things to do, but I don't want to do any of them." Real mature attitude—yes?

So I have to go back to giving myself some rules and boundaries when it comes to my time on the computer. Here are some of the rules I've imposed on myself:

1. No more than 20 minutes on Facebook a day.

I have to tell you, I loves me some Facebook.

I love seeing what old friends are up to. I love hearing about the little things in my niece's life that my brother probably wouldn't call to tell me. ("Elsa said her A-B-Cs today. We have started the Harvard Fund.") Love hearing the latest industry buzz and reading what my favorite authors and readers are up to. Love love love.

And that is where the trouble begins.

I love checking out what everyone else is up to, and I can get super caught up in commenting on people's status. That's fine when I'm standing in line at Safeway. But when I should be writing my next chapter on time management? Not so much.

So when I'm at home, I'm keeping my Facebook addiction down to 20 minutes.

2. Clear out my inbox once a week.

I will do anything to avoid answering unpleasant or complicated e-mails (see my Free Cell reference above). So I've been giving myself a weekly inbox dump where everything must be dealt with, and then I reward myself with an episode of *Top Chef*. Hey, it's better than chocolate-chip cookies.

3. Turn the wireless off for a chunk of time—every single day.

Twitter and Facebook and e-mail—oh my!

I have several ways to keep myself entertained on my computer. I love hitting the reload button on my Outlook to see what new mail I have sitting there. (Yes, we've already established I have a problem. Now let's move on, shall we?)

So, for about three hours every day, I turn off my wireless and concentrate on just working. Whether it's writing a blog post, writing a chapter, brainstorming a new speaking topic, or having a conversation with a client, I focus completely on the task at hand and not on the e-mail that I'm waiting for.

I call this my "Cave Time," and it's the only portion of the day that

I can trust myself to do anything that involves numbers or creativity (which for me, both require superhuman concentration).

Now don't get me wrong—a little Free Cell every once in a while is a good thing. But I want my computer to be a tool to get more things done instead of a distraction that keeps me from getting things done. I can watch all the cute cats on YouTube I want once my speech is written!

Maybe wasting time on your computer is not your vice. When I asked a group of women what their secret (or not-so-secret) time suckers were, here's what they came up with:

- Celebrity Gossip
- Phone time with friends
- Texting
- *Glamour* magazine
- Shopping (for self and kids)
- Looking for recipes
- "Stupid" TV
- YouTube
- Solitaire
- Twitter and Facebook

> I want my computer to be a tool to get more things done instead of a distraction that keeps me from getting things done.

All of these things, in moderation, are fine for most of us. But I know that I have let an hour of writing time turn into "just checking out a few LOLCATS pics on www.icanhascheezburger.com." Gulp.

Fear of Success

Sometimes, it can be a bit scary to start working on things we are passionate about. If we never get started, we never get disillusioned. It's a lot easier to give up on a game of Spider Solitaire or watch *Entertainment Tonight* than to get frustrated by bumping up against obstacles while working toward your goals.

I have to set up rules for myself when it comes to computer time. Is there an area of your life that you need to get under control in order to get stuff done? How will you do it—set time controls on your computer? Have a friend hold you accountable?

I've given myself a not-so-subtle reminder. Whenever I open up my computer, a quote from Benjamin Franklin pops up to remind me how I need to choose to spend my time: "Lost time is never found again."

"Lost time is never found again."

—Benjamin Franklin

Prayer for Today

Thank You for the gift of today. Help me to spend it wisely, according to Your purposes.

Getting Creative

- Have a friend set parental controls on your computer if your time wasting is truly out of hand.

- Limit yourself to ___ hours of TV a week.

- Go to Target armed with a list—and avoid the areas (kids' clothes, handbags) that suck you in.

- Set up "work hours" for yourself at home. If you ask your kids to honor that time, you'll be a lot less likely to get distracted.

- Use some of these diversions as rewards. "Once I complete my 45 minutes of study, I will give myself 15 minutes of *Vogue* magazine."

Project Reports

"I need to give up (or cut back on) not just one thing, but all my little time wasters. Facebook is certainly one of them, as is just shuffling important papers around on my desk, making innumerable lists (and then misplacing them...hence, the aforementioned shuffling), allowing my mind to make up and dwell on scenarios (complete with full conversations) most of which have never nor will ever happen. In short, I need to better discipline myself. I need to be transformed by the renewing of my mind (I think I once read that somewhere!)"—Carol

"Computer time is probably #1. I think I'm using it to avoid a lot of things."—Robin

"The one thing I'm willing to give up in order to make my goal a reality is to use my time more wisely. I'm a stay-at-home mom, and people tend to think I'm *always* available to do stuff. I'm a people pleaser, so I say yes a lot. I need to stop that and focus more on what *I need to do*!"—Kim

Your Plan for the Project *(copy your plan on* The Me Project *Planner at the back of this book)*

Results

Project 17

Laying Down Tracks
What to Do While You're Waiting

"But I want it now!"
VARUCA SALT, *Charlie and the Chocolate Factory*

Your Project

If God is telling you to wait on part or all of your goal, figure out what you can do in the meantime.

When I first started writing, I took advantage of every opportunity I could to find time to write and to learn the craft. I spent some of my lunch breaks with my writing journal, jotting down ideas for future projects. While waiting at the doctor's or dentist's office, I read writers magazines instead of *People* magazine. While driving to and from work, I listened to CDs about the writing process instead of the Top 40 station. While my kids swam at the community pool, I outlined articles and researched magazines I would like to write for someday.

When my kids were asleep, I wrote. It may have been only two sentences or an idea for something that I wanted to do someday, but I wrote. I knew that I may not finish an actual article, but I also knew it was important to lay the groundwork for the career I was dreaming of.

Was it selfish to yearn for writing time when I had so many other things going on in my life? Many people may think so. I saw it as honoring the dreams God laid on my heart.

One of the biggest challenges we have as women is assigning importance to our dreams—those desires God has planted in our heart. We figure, why spend the time now when the things we want to accomplish are so far off?

Invest

We need to make the commitment to invest in ourselves. If we have a passion to do something, whether it's open a business, write a book, or learn to dance, what is one little thing that can get us closer to accomplishing that goal?

It's time to invest, time to lay down the groundwork, so that when the season comes to live your dream, you are ready.

In one of my favorite movies, *Under the Tuscan Sun*, there is a scene where the lead character, Francis, is kicking herself for buying a villa in Tuscany. It's a big, beautiful house—perhaps too big for a woman who is single and has no children. She cries to her friend and real estate agent, Martini, "I bought a house for a life I don't even have."

Laying down track looks different for each of us.

I will never forget the words Martini encourages her with: "Signora, between Austria and Italy, there is a section of the Alps called the Semmering. It is an impossibly steep, very high part of the mountains. They built a train track over these Alps to connect Vienna and Venice. They built these tracks even before there was a train in existence that could make the trip. They built it because they knew some day, the train would come."

That is the kind of faith we need for our dreams. To know that someday, the train will come. To know that someday, we will have time to live out our dreams. To put down visible, tangible signs saying, "This is the life I'm going to lead. I am preparing the way for what is going to happen. I know that God is faithful to finish what He starts, and He is faithful to complete this in me."

Laying down track looks different for each of us. It may mean signing up for a class or subscribing to a magazine related to your passion.

For some people, it is just admitting to a friend (or even to themselves) that they do have a dream, and that they want to see it become a reality. What is the next length of track you need to lay down?

The Next Step (or Track)

Say that your dream is to become a professional photographer. What's the next step you can take to realize that dream, while still making sure that you're not robbing your family of the wife and mom they need? The logical next step might be to sign up for a photography class. Logical, but maybe not practical. What are some other teeny-tiny steps you could take, today?

Carry your digital camera everywhere. Become the official photographer for every family event, every child's birthday. Start in September by offering to snap Christmas pictures for your friends of their kids, pets, houses—whatever they want. Maybe your kid's teacher wants pictures of the next field trip. Make it known that you are the mom with the camera, and you are not afraid to use it.

Subscribe to a photography magazine and get familiar with the equipment and terminology. Instead of reading the latest chick-lit novel before going to bed, start studying up on shutter speeds.

Find a professional photographer and ask her out to lunch. As you treat her to a great pasta meal, ask her how she got started in her business. What are some of the mistakes she made, and how can you avoid them? What equipment does she use? You might even get to tag along on a job to see how the business works behind the scenes.

Pray about the opportunities God may already have brought into your life. Is your church website in need of a photographer for some picture updates? Does your friend need a headshot for a passport photo? Ask God to open your eyes and see what's waiting for you. Also, ask Him to bring new opportunities to you as you grow in your skills and knowledge.

Take a few minutes to write down what the next tracks are in your life. What are ten doable things (that take less than 20 minutes) that will move you toward your dream?

1.

2.

3.

4.

5.

6.

7.

8.

9.

10.

Prayer for Today

Lord, help me to see the opportunities where I see none.

Getting Creative

Here are 20 things you could do, right now, that don't take more than 20 minutes and will get you closer to your goal:

- Read an online article pertaining to your goal.

- Research how much an online class would cost.

- Search for a podcast of a lecture about your goal.

- Check your community college's catalog for a class pertaining to your goal. Even if you can't take the class for three years, you can at least know what's available.

- The next time you take your kids to the library, spend some time looking for books on your subject.

- See if there are any online demonstrations you can watch.

- Find a blog that's devoted to your goal.

- Start a binder where you can keep all the info on your goal.

- Sell something on eBay to help pay for supplies.

- Set up a folder on your computer dedicated to your goal.

- Clean a shelf in your garage or basement to dedicate to the "stuff" for your goal.

- Start a wish list of books and materials you need to accomplish your goal. The next time your kids/parents/husband/friend asks you what you want for your birthday/Christmas/anniversary, you'll be able to say something besides a gift card.

- Schedule 10 minutes a day on your calendar to work on your goal.

- Create a line item in your budget for your goal (discuss with your husband, if you have one!).

- Find a conference that would be worth attending and get on their mailing list for upcoming workshops and events.

- Talk about your goal with a friend that you love. Ask them to pray for you about it.

- Learn some of the basic terminology of your passion.

- Send someone in your field of interest a thank-you note for inspiring you.

- Start a blog about your passion (yes, that really can take less than 20 minutes).

- Find a local group that is dedicated to your goal.

Project Reports

"Part of my goal is getting my blog going. So yes, I blog a bit every day. I tend to sit and blog in chunks a few times a week, and then post from the drafts as needed. Some of my other goals are on hold right now, whereas others are a daily refinement!"—Amy

"Here are some things I am doing that don't take a lot of time but help me keep focused on my goals. Since I have been thinking, praying, and trying to pursue my goal of photography, I have found more and more friends who are also passionate about photography. I speak with them often and pick their brains about what equipment I should buy and how to shoot the nice photos that they shoot. I have also joined a camera club that meets once a month. The club consists of amateurs as well as professionals. The club has a monthly contest so that helps keep me focused when I'm just shooting pictures of my two children around the house or when we're at play. I also buy photography magazines so that I can flip through them on my lunch hour and get some tips. These little things help me learn piece by piece until I'm able to take time for photography classes. I feel as though I'm keeping up with my passion yet not taking time away from my family. It's a win-win situation for me at this time in my life."—Vashie

Your Plan for the Project *(copy your plan on* The Me Project *Planner at the back of this book)*

Results

Earning a Few Checkmarks on Your List

Understanding Some of the Things That Hold Us Back

"This is the day the LORD has made;
let us rejoice and be glad in it."

PSALM 118:24

Your Project

Recognize some of the mental blocks that may be holding you back from either getting started on or completing your goal. Acknowledge them and then deal with the issues.

I love a good list. I love to have a list of everything I want to get done in a day—errands I want to run and steps I need to take to get the family fed. Not only do I love making the list, I love checking things off the list. It actually gives me a little thrill. (I have read that more endorphins are released in checking something off a list than there are from smiling. I have no problem believing that.)

Do you want to know the full extent of my addiction to lists? If I complete something that is not already on that magic piece of paper, I write the item on the list and then check it off. Finally, at the end of the day, when I have accomplished everything that I can reasonably accomplish during a day, I leave the completed list in a strategic spot so that my husband can see it—looking for that outside validation that what I have accomplished during the day is worthy of recognition. I know, I need help.

The only problem with my sick and twisted little system? That one item that doesn't get done. There is usually a pattern in those undone to-do items. Here are some of the things that regularly go unchecked off:

- Taking my old clothes to the donation center
- Taking my car to the carwash
- Balancing our bank accounts
- Going to Costco
- Dusting

I get so many items done in a day: cooking dinner, writing a chapter for my book, laundry, writing a speech. Why is it that some things I just put off and put off until I just can't stand it anymore?

When I take a closer look at the list, and dig a little deeper, I can start to see some of the underlying reasons why I procrastinate.

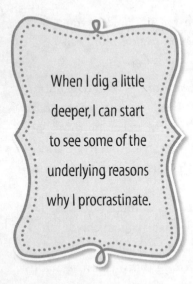

When I dig a little deeper, I can start to see some of the underlying reasons why I procrastinate.

Taking my old clothes to the donation center. A few years ago, I took a vanload of items to our local Goodwill. When I got there, the man who was receiving donations took one look at the back of my van and said in a condescending and somewhat hostile voice, "You know, we only take items in good condition. We don't accept junk."

I wanted to crawl under my minivan. Everything I was donating was in great condition; some of the clothes still had their tags on them. I never would dream of donating anything that wasn't in great shape. This man made a snap judgment—based on what? I don't know. But ever since, I have put off making a donation out of the fear of feeling shamed again.

Taking my car to the carwash. Isn't it silly that something as simple as taking my car to get washed can seem so overwhelming? Most of the speaking I do is in California, so instead of flying wherever I need to be, I usually just pack up the van. I load it with suitcases of books and props and CDs for each event. I resemble the Clampetts moving to Beverly (Hills that is. Swimming pools, movie stars…).

So when it comes to getting my car washed, I know that I first need to unload the car. But I can't just unload the car; I have to put everything away. And in putting everything away, I need to restock my book inventory for my next speaking engagement, reorder books, follow up with audience members who asked me to send them things, and so on. When I think about all that I need to do to have a clean van, it's a lot easier to just put it off.

Balancing our bank accounts. Does this one really need any explanation? Facing the reality of where our money is going, looking at some of the poor choices I've made. Really, how many shoes do I need? Apparently the answer is always, "One more pair." Reality is not a whole lot of fun.

Going to Costco. I never want to make the trip to the big box store unless I have everything prepared. Do we have a list that everyone in the family has added to? (Because there's nothing worse than coming back from a $400 shopping trip and having one of my boys say, "Why is there never anything to eat in this house?") Have I cleaned out the freezer and fridge so there's room for what we purchase? Will there be someone at home to help me unload and put away the 50-pound bag of dog food for the 25-pound dog?

As I wait for all the stars to line up, my Costco trips, which I should do about once a month, end up becoming a twice-a-year-more-planning-than-an-excursion-to-the-North-Pole nightmare.

Dusting. Hate it. Wish someone else would just do it for me.

In all of these situations, I've had to look at the underlying cause of my procrastination and find the more appropriate (i.e., the least painful) way to deal with it.

A Checklist (you know I love those) of How
to Stop Procrastinating

☐ *Break it down.*

It's so easy to become overwhelmed with a huge task—and so much easier to just put off getting started. Break your task into five-minute doable steps. Instead of putting the goal of "Write an article for the local parenting magazine" in front of you, break it down into "Spend five minutes looking at past copies of the magazine" or "Create a rough outline for the article." Make it something you could do in five minutes to feel that adrenalin rush of a checkmark.

☐ *Deal with the feelings*

If you are postponing doing a certain task because you're worried you may not do it well, or someone will criticize you for the way you're doing it, recognize it and deal with it. Now when I prepare things to take to Goodwill, I double-check each item to make sure it's something I would be fine wearing (or fine with someone I love wearing). If so, I donate with confidence, knowing that it's someone else's issue if they're not happy with my offering.

It is the same in areas of performance. We need to give ourselves permission to be messy as we grow in our skills. Not everything is going to look perfect the first time out. Make sure you show whatever you are working on to a "safe" person, someone who is going to encourage you and give you valuable, constructive feedback.

☐ *Settle for less than perfect*

If you wait until everything is perfect, you will get nothing done (or even started). Be willing to be messy in getting things done. So what if you have to go back to the library because you forgot to write down a book on your list? You probably didn't need 12 books on watercolor to get you started—11 are fine.

☐ *Imagine the worst—then do it anyway*

I put off so much stuff because of perceived fears and imagined obstacles. The reality of the situation usually turns out to be nothing like my imagined fears. I love this story from Pierce Vincent Eckhart:

> When I was a Boy Scout, we played a game when new Scouts joined the troop. We lined up chairs in a pattern, creating an obstacle course through which the new Scouts, blindfolded, were supposed to maneuver. The Scoutmaster gave them a few moments to study the pattern before our adventure began. But as soon as the victims were blindfolded, the rest of us quietly removed the chairs. I think life is like this game. Perhaps we spend our lives avoiding obstacles we have created for ourselves and in reality exist only in our minds. We're afraid to apply for that job, take violin lessons, learn a foreign language, call an old friend, write our Congressman—whatever it is that we would really like to do but don't because of perceived obstacles. Don't avoid any chairs until you run smack into one. And if you do, at least you'll have a place to sit down.

☐ *Quiet the voices*

If you are convinced that the next step is the one you're supposed to take, don't worry about what others are going to say if it doesn't turn out. So what if your dad told you that you were not graceful—take that beginner tap class and thoroughly enjoy every step of it. Have you always told yourself that you are not artistic, but you would love to know how to design websites? A lot of the artistic stuff is inborn talent, but a lot of it is just plain knowing the "rules" of art—balance and color can, to a large extent, be taught. Your work may never hang in the Louvre, but your favorite nonprofit might just be thrilled to have your unique touch on their website.

Prayer for Today

Lord, help me to finish well today.

Getting Creative

If one item is hanging you up, try one of the following to get it done:

- Call a friend and ask her to check in with you to see if you got your chore done.

- Post it on Facebook—that way you'll have a whole community holding you accountable.

- Combine with a friend—if you both despise the same activity—and make a day out of it with a reward at the end (quick manicure? coffee?).

Project Reports

"As far back as high school I remember my mom's sage advice, 'Don't wish your life away.' I often wished time would pass quickly so I could be done with whatever situation was bogging me down. It was easier to ignore the irksome details of daily life while anticipating something better to come. Whether it was denial or simple avoidance, it was a habit I continued for years.

"In college, I was sure happiness would be mine once I survived the current semester and started new classes. Throughout my career I switched jobs every few years due to discontent. And when I got married, it became extremely easy to be forward-focused as my husband climbed the corporate ladder. With each new job came fresh opportunities for true happiness (a different city, house, job, friends). I just knew that the next time we moved I would finally be content. Next time.

"Well, after my first child was born, I longed for the normal routine of life before kids. That's when I finally realized chasing happiness was futile. I wasted years searching for contentment everywhere except the very places God had put me.

"While the temptation to overlook today's issues for tomorrow's blessing occasionally still tugs at me, I'm much better at living in the moment. I wish I could've learned this sooner: God knows best. My purpose, my peace, my joy... all of it can be found by living the life God designed for me... today."—Teresa

Your Plan for the Project *(copy your plan on* The Me Project *Planner at the back of this book)*

Results

Project 19

What Color Is Your Belt?
Making Milestones Along the Way

*"It is important that you recognize your progress
and take pride in your accomplishments.
Share your achievements with others. Brag a little.
The recognition and support of those around you is nurturing."*

Rosemarie Rossetti

Your Project

Figure out a tangible way to remember—and celebrate—how far God has taken you in living out your dream.

For most of us, it's easy to see how much further we have to go to reach our goal, but hard to remember how far God has already brought us.

I love how the prophet Samuel set up a reminder for the people of Israel when God rescued them from their Philistine oppressors: "Then Samuel took a stone and set it up between Mizpah and Shen. He named it Ebenezer, saying, 'Thus far has the LORD helped us'" (1 Samuel 7:12).

Physical reminders of God's love and provision are important in our lives. Whether it's rocks in our garden, diaries filled with a record of God's miracles in our lives, or photo albums filled with reminders, it's important to keep track of God's blessings. That way, when we feel He's distant, we can be reminded that God is concerned for our every thought and need.

I also believe in commemorating how far God has brought you.

Whether you are well on the road to recognizing your dream or just taking first steps as you think, plan, and dream, God has done a lot of work to get you to this place.

Accessories as Recognition

I am very jealous of my friend Kathy. Kathy has decided to take up martial arts. She goes to a dojo several times a week, practices sparring, and sometimes comes home black and blue (and I'm not referring to the colors of her belt).

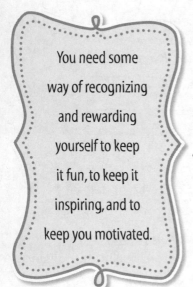

You need some way of recognizing and rewarding yourself to keep it fun, to keep it inspiring, and to keep you motivated.

But that's not why I'm jealous. I'm jealous because Kathy gets tangible markers of where she is on her journey. You always know what belt Kathy is working on. She has a piece of material that says, "Hey, I've worked hard and accomplished something!"

I wish they gave out accessories for some of my goals.

I wish that each time I finished a chapter of a book, I would get a different colored scarf.

Or every time I created a new retreat, I would get a different pair of earrings.

So I need to come up with my own markers—places to record and even celebrate the small (and big) steps as I take them every day.

Reward Systems Rock

Karate has its belts. Weight Watchers has its pins and ribbons. College has its diplomas. Organizations know that rewarding progress keeps you coming back. So if you are not part of an organization, how do you reward your progress? You need some way of recognizing and rewarding yourself to keep it fun, to keep it inspiring, and to keep you motivated.

I know some people will say, "The satisfaction of doing a good job is reward enough." I imagine these people have never enjoyed a good massage or a piece of Godiva chocolate. (You can see why I struggle so much in the weight department.)

So here are some noncaloric ways to celebrate your progress as you work toward your goals:

Excel spreadsheets. A good checkmark can go a long way. When I'm writing a book, I put each chapter onto a line of the spreadsheet and keep up-to-date on the word count. It makes me really excited to see my number of words growing bigger and bigger.

Charts on your wall. If gold stars can motivate kids, how much more as an adult do I need something that says, "Good job!"

Handbags (or whatever your equivalent is). Many of the writers I know spend their book advances on such exotic and fun things as food, shelter, and utilities. However, many of them have a designer-bag fetish that compels them to write almost as much as feeding their families and keeping the lights on. It's fun to run into Shelley and know that her grass-green Kate Spade bag is the result of the six-book contract she scored last year.

Girlfriend time. When I'm on a writing deadline, showering becomes optional. This is when I go into "cave mode" and cut the telephone chitchat and stop going to brunch with my buddies. So, part of my reward system includes spending some nongoal-focused time with my girls.

The dog park. OK, this may seem weird, but both my dog and I love going to the local dog park. He gets to run around like a wild banshee, and I get to accomplish nothing for an hour.

TV. I definitely have some guilty-pleasure programming that's a great reward for knocking off small things from my list. *30 Rock* anyone?

Swap rewards. My son and I do this often. If I get my goal checked off, he buys Starbucks. If he gets his stuff accomplished, it's my treat. And on the days when we both meet our goals? I still treat. I'm the mom after all.

Three Rules for Tracking Your Progress

1. Put it where you can see it.

I hang mine in my charts in the bathroom—it's the first thing I see in the morning, and the last thing at night…

2. Small steps count.

At my recent Weight Watchers meeting, one of the attendees was overwhelmed by frustration because she had lost only two ounces. The leader who was weighing her in, a woman who had lost over 50 pounds and had kept them off for over 20 years, said to her, "Honey, I didn't lose my weight in pounds. I lost it in ounces." Here is a woman who was inarguably a success in the goal she accomplished, but had done it very, very slowly.

3. Big steps really count.

Make sure you don't downplay when you do something big and scary and brave. When I get an advance for a book, we use that to live off of, but we also do a treat for the whole family. One time it was a two-day trip to Disneyland; another was dinner out at our favorite Italian place. This way, my whole family gets to celebrate with me, and I get to share with them.

Prayer for Today

Help me to see Your hand guiding me through this process and to recognize Your provision for me in everything that I do.

Getting Creative

- When I first started writing, my friend Lynn and I would swap goals, and when we hit those goals, we would send each other stickers. It may seem silly, but I really looked forward to getting those stickers as tangible proof that I had written a chapter, written an article, or accomplished some other writing goal.

- Find contests to enter. My fellow coffee-shop writers, Cathy and Katie, have both entered (and won) major writing contests. Besides the recognition and confirmation that they are great at what they do, these contests have provided a shorter-term goal to the big goal—getting their books finished.

- A charm bracelet or necklace would be a great way to celebrate the little steps of your goal along the way.

Project Reports

"I am trying to do something related to art every week—usually after all the kids are in bed. I need to keep at it or weeks turn into months into years. When I pay for a class I hold myself more accountable, so that really helps. I also try to enter art shows when there is an opportunity."—Sandra

Your Plan for the Project *(copy your plan on* The Me Project *Planner at the back of this book)*

Results

Project 20

Are We Having Fun Yet?
Joy for the Journey

"Do not run through life so fast that you
forget not only where you have been,
but also where you are going."

Author unknown

Your Project

Make sure that even if you haven't reached your goal, you are
having some fun along the way. Not only will that make it easier to work at, it will keep you motivated as well.

"Off to Weight Watchers. I don't think they give out ribbons for my
kind of weight change…"

That's what I posted on Facebook one Thursday morning before
returning to the weekly meeting I'd been skipping regularly. Within an
hour, I had two people ask me which meeting I go to and if I would be
there the following week. Within a day, the number was up to six.

The following Thursday, I sat at the meeting with two friends, Kathy
and Carrie, who were also committing to count points for the rest of
their lives. Each of them said the same thing: "I've tried it on my own
and it hasn't worked. The only way I've ever had any success is by doing
this with a friend."

The other reason I love this meeting so much? It's *fun*. I know, there
really isn't much about weight loss that's a real knee-slapper, but you
know what? I look forward to going to this group. The instructor is
real—she talks about her own struggles and can laugh at herself. The

other members have a sense of humor about their outrageous desires to put butter on everything.

Do I love thinking about my weight all the time? No. Am I still going to meetings? Yes. Because I look forward to it.

In the past, I have spent a lot of time dreaming about what I would do once I lost the weight, wrote a book, was financially stable, and so on. But part of sticking with a plan is learning to live with and actually enjoy the plan—not just waiting to start my life once I've achieved my goal.

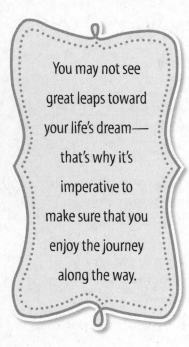

You may not see great leaps toward your life's dream— that's why it's imperative to make sure that you enjoy the journey along the way.

You may not see great leaps toward your life's dream—that's why it's imperative to make sure that you enjoy the journey along the way.

For Christmas, my brother and his wife gave Roger and me a weekend away in beautiful Big Sur, California. Big Sur is south of Monterey on the central California coastline. With its craggy cliffs and pristine beaches, it's one of the most beautiful spots in the world.

I had plenty of books, magazines, CDs, and notepads to keep me busy on the trip to the resort. I was anxious to get our vacation started and desperately wanted to get to our hotel with the ocean view. As Roger leisurely cruised up Highway 1, I silently wished he would get the lead out so we could start to enjoy our resort.

Finally, after several hours moseying along, I had had enough.

"Honey, do you think we could go a little faster? The retirees towing their fifth wheel stopped, had lunch, and just passed us again."

Roger looked at me in astonishment. "Are you kidding? This is the best part of the vacation! Look at the scenery, look at the ocean. I just want to drink it all in—I don't want to miss any of it."

I spend a lot of time dreaming about my life when all the kids are grown. I will no longer be the 24-hour taxi service. Cooking for two adults with grown-up palates will be so much easier than cooking for four picky kids. I long for the day that I come home and not trip over multiple backpacks by the front door.

And yet, I worry that with all my wishing, I am sometimes missing the best part. Many people have given me the advice, "Stop and smell the roses." In this case, it seems my roses are three teenagers and young adults living at home in different states of cleanliness. While I may not want to smell them most of the time, I do want to enjoy the time that they are under my care.

Find ways to make reaching for your goals a process that you can embrace and support.

This book is designed to give you a foundation to accomplish whatever God has laid on your heart. But let's be realistic: You are probably not going to accomplish your goal in 21 days. I want you to enjoy the journey, not assume that your life begins when you become a full-time photographer or launch that graphic design business.

What part of pursuing your goal are you really enjoying right now?

Prayer for Today

Today, Lord, I want to experience everything You have for me. I want to enjoy the process of getting to my goals instead of just waiting to start my life when I accomplish my goals.

Getting Creative

- One of the things I have done for writing is create a soundtrack for each book. I so look forward to popping in my earphones every day. It makes me feel like a real writer.

- Have some travel buddies along the way that keep it fun. Limit naysayers in your life (or, if you are related to said naysayers, limit how much you share with them).

Project Reports

"I take classes and hang with people who are good at what I like to do. I'm a member of guilds that are into sewing as a passion and for fun. I found some of the guilds online and some through friends. The benefits? Fun, networking, friendship, and knowledge. Anytime you learn something about your chosen goal, it gets you closer to realizing it. Being around other creative people just inspires me to be more creative!"
—Regena

Your Plan for the Project *(copy your plan on* The Me Project *Planner at the back of this book)*

Results

Bumps, Craters, and Goo in the Road
Pushing Through When Things Don't Go According to Plan

"All the adversity I've had in my life,
all my troubles and obstacles have strengthened me…
You may not realize it when it happens,
but a kick in the teeth may be the best thing in the world for you."

WALT DISNEY

Your Project

Anticipate that things are going to go wrong—and then have a plan to deal with it.

My husband is an easygoing guy—until you get him near any Disney park. He becomes a man obsessed.

You see, I *like* Disney. I enjoy going to Disneyland. (Disney World is something else entirely. Who decided to build a theme park in hot, muggy Florida? But I digress.)

Roger knows his Disney trivia. He knows when the "Small World" ride was created (1964), the original price of admission ($1), when Disneyland stopped using e-tickets (1982), and how many teacups you can make your wife sick in by spinning too fast (18). Before we were married, he would journey to the promised land of Mickey and Minnie three or four times a year. If someone working at Disney tries to give Roger directions or asks if we need help, he becomes slightly insulted.

So it was a no-brainer what I was going to do for Roger's birthday. I heard on the radio that a museum in Oakland was hosting an exhibit, "Behind the Magic—50 Years of Disneyland." I ordered the tickets, made reservations at a restaurant near the museum, and planned a few other surprises for the day.

It was everything that I hoped for. The exhibit provided all the behind-the-scenes nerdy Disney trivia that I knew Roger would love. In one room were vintage newsreels of Uncle Walt introducing Disneyland to the rest of the world. On display in another section of the museum were the original sketches and plans for Disneyland, all with notations and scribbles from Walt Disney himself. In another room, you could see some of the original employee handbooks with style and grooming requirements. Toward the end of the exhibit, you could see one of my favorites, one of the original cars from "Mr. Toad's Wild Ride."

The further you got into the event, the more you realized what a genius Walt Disney was. Not only was he a visionary, but he knew how to make his vision a reality. He was the driving force behind everything we saw in that museum.

But one of the most interesting parts of the exhibit was the section about the opening weekend of Disneyland. On Sunday, July 17, 1955, 15,000 invited guests arrived, along with 90 million people who were invited in by way of live TV coverage. But along with the invited guests, over 8000 gate crashers climbed fences or produced forged tickets to gain entry. Along with overcrowding in the park, the Disneyland staff faced several more obstacles on the day that has come to be known as "Black Sunday."

- Local police dubbed the seven-mile freeway backup the worst mess they had ever seen.

- Rides and attractions broke down under the onslaught of guests, opening and closing periodically to make way for television crews.

- Fantasyland closed temporarily due to a gas leak.

- Main Street's freshly poured asphalt softened in the heat. Women wearing high heels sometimes left a shoe behind, stuck in black goo.

- Because of a plumber's strike, both restrooms and drinking fountains could not be ready by opening day. Walt opted for restrooms, leaving visitors hot and thirsty.

- Most reviewers declared the park overpriced and poorly managed, expecting Disneyland history to be over almost as soon as it began.

Almost every news reporter that day predicted failure for Walt and the rest of the Disney Empire.

But Walt Disney persevered. He regrouped his team, addressed the issues that plagued the opening day, and invited the press back to see all the changes that had been made. Disneyland went on to be not only the most successful theme park in history; it changed the way families around the world vacationed.

As a woman pursuing your dreams and goals, I bet you feel as though you have a lot of "Black Sundays"—those days where everything seems to go wrong. Days where you start to question, *Am I really doing the right thing? If this is God's plan for my life, shouldn't it be easier?*

Somehow we have gotten the notion that when things go right, when times are easy, we must be in God's will. But when things are hard, when there are obstacles and challenges and the kids are being monstrous, we must be going down the wrong path.

Where did we ever get such a notion? Jesus said, "I have told you these things, so that in me you may have peace. In this world you will have trouble. But take heart! I have overcome the world" (John 16:33).

One thing that you learn in life: Anything worth doing is hard.

In my previous job as a manager, I assigned tasks according to who had the strengths (skills) that best matched the work required. If an event needed to be organized, Lise was the one to do it. She could organize international peace talks if given a spreadsheet and enough coffee. If a document needed proofreading, Jane was the go-to girl. She could find mistakes in the dictionary given enough time. Since I know that I am a disorganized dyslexic, the ability to assign work to more talented people made my job much easier.

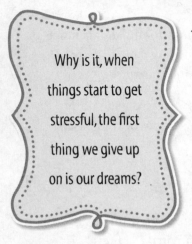

Why is it, when things start to get stressful, the first thing we give up on is our dreams?

When pursuing your goals, however, rarely can you assign the work to someone else. You are the woman who has to get your son to his voice lessons, your daughter to church, and dinner to your friend who just had a baby, all at 5:00—after a long day at work. And somehow you do it. You wouldn't let a little thing like the space/time continuum interrupt your schedule. You just plow through and make it happen.

So why is it, when things in our lives start to get stressful, the first thing we give up on is our dreams?

It is the hardest thing in the world to keep going after your goals when it feels as if other things in your life are falling apart. Money is tight—there are more bills than dollars. Time is tight—you are not giving up just television at this point, you are giving up sleep. Often, when life is tough, it may seem that the best decision is to put aside your own desires in order to concentrate on whatever problem is in front of you.

So, how do you stay on task when life is hard?

Run to God, Every Day

The most vital thing you can do when encountering problems is to run to God, every day.

Trying to pursue dreams and raise kids at the same time is difficult. But the knowledge that you are on God's path for your life can help you handle some of those bumpy roads. We are never alone. Whether it is mothering or accomplishing our goals, God is there guiding us, supporting us, and making a way for us.

> Cast your cares on the LORD
> and he will sustain you;
> he will never let the righteous fall.
>   (Psalm 55:22)

It has been my experience that when God asks you to do big things, He shows up in big ways. When you have a problem in front of you—be sure to use all your strength.

Your Goals Are Designed to Give You Strength, Not Zap Your Energy

When Roger and I were first married, the challenges of putting together a stepfamily could sometimes be overwhelming. That's a nice way of saying that despite all the counseling we did and the books we read, we felt totally ill-prepared and unequipped. While Roger and I are both committed Christians and want to follow God's plan for raising our kids, it looked as though we had two separate sets of blueprints.

"The best prayers often have more groans than words."

—John Bunyan

I was what I considered a "relaxed" parent—and then I married Roger. He makes Winnie the Pooh look downright uptight. I was crying out for more structure. We spent the months before our wedding and the first year of our marriage in discussions and prayer on how to meld these two very different households.

There were many times I wanted to put my own desires aside. I made the decision at several points to give up my book club, writing, and other activities that I loved. I just thought I should spend all my time working on putting together my new family.

Roger, however, insisted that I keep doing some of those things that would get me closer to my goals, and that I enjoyed. He knew that when life at home was trying, the friends at my book club or the other ladies at the gym where I worked out gave me support and encouragement. They were a vital link to my sanity at a very stressful time.

He later admitted that he didn't do it just for me. He knew there were two key ingredients to keeping me sane: friends and coffee. He said it was in the entire family's best interest that he keep me well supplied in both.

As women, we need our support systems around us. We need people who can be our refuge and can help us pray through the tough times.

I have also found that it's important to have friends who are survivors. Some people have seen a lot of heartache in their lives and have lived to tell the story.

Keep Your Focus

When you start to get discouraged, make sure you keep your eye on your goal down the road, not on the pothole in front of you.

This is the area that I have learned a lot from my daughter. She is one of the hardest working people I know. In any area where she lacks natural ability, she makes up for it in dogged persistence.

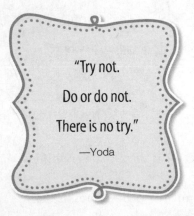

"Try not.
Do or do not.
There is no try."

—Yoda

When her PE class was learning badminton, she wanted to buy—using her own money—a badminton racket and birdie to practice serving. When it was volleyball, she would try to coax family members to go out on the front lawn and throw volleyballs at her (for some reason, her brother kept volunteering for the job). She is the girl who will handwrite flyers to pass out door-to-door to start her own dog-sitting business. That she had never owned a dog did not deter her. She never gives up.

When problems come up, do you let them throw you, or do you figure a way to get through them? Maybe it takes thinking about the problem in a new way or consulting an expert in the field. The important thing is to stick to it. Have faith that what God has called you to, He has equipped you for.

Prayer for Today

Lord, help me to recognize You in every step of this journey and to lean on You for strength to make it through.

Getting Creative

- Quotes and Bible verses can go a long way in helping you stay focused on your goal when things get hard. Roger and I use our master bathroom to put up verses, our goals, quotes that keep us on track, and notes of encouragement to each other.

- Be sure to share your struggles not only with God but with a friend who will remind you of all you have overcome in the past.

- Look back at Project 1. See all the ways that God has led you on this path.

Project Reports

"When I get discouraged, God has surrounded me with a wonderful group of solid Christian women who bless me, encourage me, and spur me on. Ultimately, however, I am finding that *Christ alone* is my single biggest Advocate and Mentor."—Jane

Your Plan for the Project *(copy your plan on* The Me Project *Planner at the back of this book)*

Results

The End (and the Beginning)
of *The Me Project*

I'm excited that you got to the end of your journey, at least as far as the book is concerned. You may not have reached your goal yet (and really, that's OK!), but I'm guessing you're a whole lot closer than when you started.

I'm also guessing that you made some discoveries along the way:

- Maybe you discovered you were closer than you thought to accomplishing your goal.

- Maybe you found some new people who share your passion.

- Maybe your goal took a different direction than you expected.

- Maybe God showed you some things about yourself that you hadn't expected.

- Maybe God told you to wait on this goal.

- Maybe you will have to make some big changes to follow the path God is laying out for you.

These are all great outcomes.

The whole purpose of *The Me Project* is to get you closer to who God designed you to be. If that means putting your goal on hold—or realizing it was never your goal in the first place—that is better than OK. That is God speaking to you and shaping you.

It may seem that some of the other women in your group got a lot farther down the road toward their goal than you did. Can I give you a piece of advice? Don't compare. Any step you take toward getting closer to the plan God has for you is holy progress.

What's Next?

Keep this book nearby. You're going to have other goals to work through and dreams to accomplish. Refer back to this book the next time you and some friends want to make a change.

Plus, keep updating that 50/50 journal. You'll be amazed at how God is growing you and your dreams over the years—and grateful at remembering how God is working in your life (sometimes when you don't see or understand fully what is going on).

Finally, be sure to stop by the website www.ProjectsForYourSoul.com, and share your story with other Project Managers. Who knows, maybe you will read someone else's story that will ignite your next God-given goal!

Tools of
The Me Project

The Me Project Planner

Here is the place for you to put down your plans for *The Me Project*. If you are anything like me, you are a girl who loves a checklist—and here's a checklist for your goal.

As you read through the chapters, be sure to make notes here in *The Me Project* Planner about what you want to do. Be intentional, be consistent, and you will see results.

If it's easier for you to make a copy of these pages, feel free. I want it to be as user-friendly as possible.

- Write down one or two sentences about what your plan is for each day.

- Make copies of this plan to share with your accountability partners to help keep you on track.

- Make some extra copies for yourself. Leave one at the office, one in your purse or daily planner, and one in your Bible. That way, no matter where you are, you'll know what your project is for today and be able to plan to create some time.

- As you complete the projects, make sure you give yourself a checkmark on your planner. Nothing feels quite as satisfying on a busy day as a "project accomplished" checkmark.

Week One

Sunday: Project 1   ☐ check when completed
Your plan for the project:

Monday: Project 2   ☐ check when completed
Your plan for the project:

Tuesday: Project 3   ☐ check when completed
Your plan for the project:

Wednesday: Project 4   ☐ check when completed
Your plan for the project:

Thursday: Project 5   ☐ check when completed
Your plan for the project:

Friday: Project 6   ☐ check when completed
Your plan for the project:

Saturday: Project 7   ☐ check when completed
Your plan for the project:

Week Two

Sunday: Project 8   ☐ check when completed
Your plan for the project:

Monday: Project 9   ☐ check when completed
Your plan for the project:

Tuesday: Project 10   ☐ check when completed
Your plan for the project:

Wednesday: Project 11   ☐ check when completed
Your plan for the project:

Thursday: Project 12   ☐ check when completed
Your plan for the project:

Friday: Project 13   ☐ check when completed
Your plan for the project:

Saturday: Project 14   ☐ check when completed
Your plan for the project:

Week Three

Sunday: Project 15   ☐ check when completed
Your plan for the project:

Monday: Project 16   ☐ check when completed
Your plan for the project:

Tuesday: Project 17   ☐ check when completed
Your plan for the project:

Wednesday: Project 18   ☐ check when completed
Your plan for the project:

Thursday: Project 19   ☐ check when completed
Your plan for the project:

Friday: Project 20   ☐ check when completed
Your plan for the project:

Saturday: Project 21   ☐ check when completed
Your plan for the project:

Recommended Resources

Understanding God's Plan for Your Life

So Long, Status Quo: What I Learned from Women Who Changed the World by Susy Flory

When a Woman Discovers Her Dream: Finding God's Purpose for Your Life by Cindi McMenamin

Me, Myself and Bob: A True Story About Dreams, God and Talking Vegetables by Phil Vischer

The Life You've Always Wanted: Spiritual Disciplines for Ordinary People by John Ortberg

Achieving Your Goals

The Creative Life: A Workbook for Unearthing the Christian Imagination by Alice Bass

The Power of a Positive No: How to Say No and Still Get to Yes by William Ury

The Imagineering Workout by the Disney Imagineers

Getting Things Done: The Art of Stress-Free Productivity by David Allen

Ready for Anything: 52 Productivity Principles for Getting Things Done by David Allen

Write It Down, Make It Happen: Knowing What You Want and Getting It by Henriette Anne Klauser

Dear Reader,

Thanks for being a part of *The Me Project*. One of the greatest privileges I have is to hear back from the people who have used my books. I would love to stay in touch.

On the web: www.KathiLipp.com
E-mail: Kathi@ProjectsForYourSoul.com
Facebook: facebook.com/kathilipp
Twitter: twitter.com/kathilipp

Mail: Kathi Lipp
       171 Branham Lane
       Suite 10-122
       San Jose, CA 95136

- Opportunities for input and discussion with other readers are available at www.ProjectsForYourSoul.com

- If you are leading a group in *The Me Project*, check out the "For Leaders" section at www.ProjectsForYourSoul.com

In His Grace,

Kathi Lipp

The Husband Project
21 Days of Loving Your Man—
on Purpose and with a Plan

Have you and your husband gone from over-the-top romantics to tolerant roommates?

Do you dress up more to go out to dinner with your girlfriends than you do to go out with your husband?

Have you forgotten the fine art of flirting with your guy?

Maybe it's time to put your husband on Project Status.

In *The Husband Project*, Kathi Lipp shows you how, even in the midst of your busy schedule, you can take your marriage from *ordinary* to *amazing* in just 21 days. Through simple daily action plans, you'll discover fun and creative ways to bring back that lovin' feeling…and to remind you and your guy why you got married in the first place.

So rise to the challenge that women across the U.S. have taken: three weeks of putting your husband before kids, housework, jobs…and even *shopping*.

Also by Kathi Lipp:

The Marriage Project
21 Days to More Love and Laughter

More love, more laughter—more lingerie.

What would marriages look like if for 21 days, husbands and wives put their marriage on *project status*? Plenty of books describe how to improve marriage, how to save a marriage, and how to ramp up the intimacy in a marriage. In *The Marriage Project*, Kathi Lipp shows readers how to put the *fun* back in marriage with 21 simple yet effective projects, such as doing something they enjoyed together before they got married or flirting with their spouse via e-mail or text messages.

Each of the projects contains:

- a project description
- suggestions for how to complete the project
- reports from other couples on how they accomplished the project
- a prayer
- a place to record project results

In addition to the daily projects, three bonus projects encourage couples to turn up the heat in the bedroom.

For couples who haven't given up on the dream of being head-over-heels with their spouse again, *The Marriage Project* provides just the right boost.

Included are tips on how to use *The Marriage Project* to revitalize marriages in a local church or small group.

To learn more about other Harvest House books
or to read sample chapters, log on to our website:

www.harvesthousepublishers.com

HARVEST HOUSE PUBLISHERS

EUGENE, OREGON